SUPER
PULSES

First published in the United Kingdom in 2019 by
Pavilion, An imprint of HarperCollinsPublishers Ltd
1 London Bridge Street
London SE1 9GF

www.harpercollins.co.uk

HarperCollinsPublishers
Macken House
39/40 Mayor Street Upper
Dublin 1
D01 C9W8
Ireland

ISBN 978-1-911624-12-7

This book is produced from independently certified FSC™
paper to ensure responsible forest management.

For more information visit:
www.harpercollins.co.uk/green

A CIP catalogue record for this book is available from
the British Library

10 9 8 7 6 5 4 3 2

Printed and bound in Malaysia by Papercraft

Neither the author nor the publisher can accept responsibility
for any injury or illness that may arise as a result of following
the advice contained in this work. Any application of the
information contained in the book is at the reader's sole
discretion.

The oven temperatures listed within this book are for
conventional ovens. If using a fan oven, reduce the heat by
20°C. Be aware that oven temperatures may vary.

SUPER PULSES

Jenny Chandler

PAVILION

Introduction

Pulses, or legumes, are some of my favourite things to eat, and that's after a year and a half of cooking and consuming them almost every day. Yes, you would hope that I'd be passionate about my subject, but my family had no choice in the matter as they became my guinea pigs. So you just can't imagine how thrilled I was when, after months of legume exposure, my six-year-old daughter opted for the Syrian lentils on a restaurant menu. Legumes are some of the most versatile, delicious and rewarding ingredients in the kitchen. I want to eat pulses firstly because they taste fabulous; all the other plus points, and there are so many of them, come as a bonus.

At last the pulse has emerged from its tie-dye teepee. Beans, chickpeas and lentils are still the mainstay of many vegan and vegetarian diets, but attitudes and styles have changed. Plant-based food has become so varied and exciting with all the Mediterranean, Middle Eastern and Asian influences we enjoy today, it's worlds apart from the wholemeal bean flan of old. Legumes can be stars in their own right and not just a meat substitute. Why stuff beans in a moussaka when you could be eating a classic Greek vegetarian dish, *gigantes plaki*?

Nowadays many great restaurants, such as London's Ottolenghi, Moro, Petersham Nurseries, Polpo, St John and Leon, serve up wonderful legumes. Who would have believed that the humble lentil could become trendy? But then camping has dumped its nylon-cagoule image and reinvented itself as glamping, and even that swirly kaftan of your mother's has become boho-chic. I believe our passion for pulses is much more than a fashion. The pulse is real food and it's here to stay.

Most of us are reassessing what we eat for a number of reasons, the first being money. Reducing what you spend on food needn't mean buying cheap junk food, it just requires some planning and good recipes that you actually use. Pulses are remarkably cheap, especially if you buy them dried – but if you're short of time, even canned pulses are very economical. Gingery dal with a spiced tarka tipped over the top, served with some rice or flatbread, is one of my favourite suppers ever and it costs a matter of pence.

I'm not vegetarian but, like so many people I know, I am eating less meat. Instead of having cheap meat every day, I'd much rather eat more expensive but better meat once a week, or in smaller quantities alongside my pulses, knowing that the animal it came from was healthy and well treated. Enjoying fabulous legume dishes, packed with plant-based protein, comes with no sense of deprivation and is quite simply more environmentally friendly. Fish is a treat, but there are sustainability issues too and it can be very pricey. However, you can savour a small but exquisite, carefully sourced bit of seafood with some filling pulses and feel perfectly satisfied.

Pulses are, without a doubt, wonderfully good for you and, with cases of obesity reaching record levels, we really do need to rethink what we're consuming. I love food and I love cooking, so I quite naturally gravitate towards simple unadulterated ingredients. Legumes, whether dried, canned or frozen, are just that; you know what you are getting.

Using the Recipes

Wherever possible, I've given a choice between using home-cooked and canned pulses. I recognize the need for dishes that you can fling together in a few minutes after work and the fact that boiling up an entire pot of beans just doesn't make sense if you're cooking for one. However, where dishes absolutely rely on the pulses absorbing stocks or flavours, I have only suggested using dried. Many of the beans in these recipes can be interchanged, even if the bean police (and they are out there) get a bit upset about it.

Note: When using canned beans and lentils, be sure to drain and rinse them really well.

The Power of the Pulse

One of the great things about eating legumes is that you can feel good about yourself in body, mind and spirit. It's not just that these little wonder seeds are fantastically nutritious and packed with healthy fibre, they could help us save the planet too. While I'm determined not to leap on my soapbox, it is really important to realize just what valuable and under-exploited ingredients pulses are.

What's in it for me?

Nutritionists are increasingly seeing pulses as one of the great weapons against obesity, diabetes, heart disease and cancer. Pulses have plenty of good complex carbohydrates loaded with fibre. They are relatively high in protein, low in fat and packed with nutrients, especially iron, calcium, zinc, potassium, and B vitamins.

Carbs and fibre

Starchy carbs (as opposed to the sugary ones) are the body's healthiest source of energy and should ideally supply about half of our daily calories.

Foods with high levels of fibre are not just filling at meal times but also make you feel full for much longer, so that you're unlikely to dive into the biscuit tin within a few hours of eating. This satiated feeling is closely linked to the speed at which our blood sugar levels rise and fall after eating certain foods, which are measured on the glycaemic index (GI). Pulses have a low GI, meaning that they produce a steady rise and equally steady fall of blood glucose levels instead of the peaks and troughs that can have you snacking. So, eating plenty of pulses is really helpful if you want to lose weight or maintain a healthy diet. Pulses can also be significant in preventing or managing type 2 diabetes.

Hot-smoked salmon, egg and lentil salad (see page 82)

While the fibre slows down the absorption of sugars, it also speeds up the passage of food through your body, accelerating the removal of toxins and excess cholesterol and keeping you regular, reducing the risk of colon and bowel cancer.

High protein

We all need protein in our diet: it's one of the building blocks of the human body, in our nerves, tissues and bones. It's necessary for growth and repair and the production of hormones, enzymes and even the antibodies that fight off viruses, bacteria and toxins. Pulses can provide the highest levels of protein in the plant world.

Proteins are made up of amino acids, some of which our bodies are able to make themselves and nine of which we need to absorb from our food. Whereas meat, fish, dairy and eggs can provide all nine amino acids, pulses are lacking in some, methionine in particular. Soya beans are the only exception: they are a source of 'complete' or 'high- quality' protein. However, in one of those miracles of nature, grains, nuts and seeds can provide the last piece of the jigsaw. There's no need to consciously combine these complementary ingredients within a meal, it's just a question of eating a varied diet with a good mix of these protein sources, particularly if you are vegan or vegetarian.

Low fat, no cholesterol

As most of us are aware, pulses can be a very important source of protein – but many of us eat plenty of protein anyway. However, increasingly, we're all being encouraged to substitute some of our meat and dairy intake with legumes. Dairy and meat products contain varying levels of saturated fat and cholesterol while most pulses are low in fat (and most of that's unsaturated) and are cholesterol free. Soya beans and peanuts are the exceptions, being higher in fat, but that's predominantly unsaturated 'good' fats. Our bodies need cholesterol but, to put it simply, there's good and bad cholesterol; saturated fats are loaded with bad cholesterol that can clog up your blood vessels. By cutting back on saturated fats, you can reduce the risk of strokes, heart attacks and all the other forms of cardiovascular disease.

The other fats to avoid are the trans fats found in much processed, and commercially fried, food. These hydrogenated fats play havoc with cholesterol levels, so go for natural oils and fats with your beans and eliminate trans fats altogether.

The low-fat/high-fibre credentials of the legume make it a good contender for a weight-loss diet: filling and low fat, what could be better? Just remember to watch what you eat your pulses with and maybe halve the number of sausages in the casserole!

Minerals, vitamins and the rest of the good news

Legumes are good sources of calcium, magnesium and phosphorous, which are all vital in the formation and health of bones and teeth, especially critical during childhood and adolescence. These minerals are also required for muscle function, blood clotting, nerve reactions, normalizing blood sugar levels, lowering blood pressure and maintaining a healthy immune system.

Pulses have healthy levels of potassium, which is particularly helpful in lowering blood pressure, balancing out the negative effects of too much salt, and helping the kidneys work more efficiently.

Legumes are high in zinc, crucial for a healthy immune system and healing wounds; it's also said to improve fertility and libido. Many of us absorb a large proportion of our zinc from meat, so if you are vegetarian, do make sure that you eat plenty of pulses, nuts and seeds.

Pulses do contain plenty of iron, a particularly important consideration for vegetarians. However, unlike the more accessible iron found in meat, this 'non-haem' iron is more difficult for the body to assimilate, so you will need to combine your legumes with foods rich in vitamin C in order to absorb it effectively. No problem, as long as you are eating some fresh vegetables or salad alongside your pulses – and don't underestimate the power of a good squeeze of lemon juice or a generous sprinkling of fresh parsley.

Fresh peas and beans are also high in vitamin C, which protects the body against respiratory infections, skin diseases and cardiovascular problems. Although, for the purposes of this book I have concentrated mainly on dried peas and beans.

Pulses are good sources of many B vitamins, which help to convert carbohydrates into energy. Folic acid, or folate as it is also known, is essential for healthy red blood cells; it is probably best known for reducing the risk of central nervous system defects (notably spina bifida) in unborn babies. Niacin is another important B vitamin that helps the body produce hormones and is also believed to reduce levels of bad cholesterol.

Pulses are now recognized to have many other health benefits too. They contain antioxidants that help to neutralize free radicals (chemicals that damage cells in the body and lead to ageing and disease). The saponins found in pulses may reduce your risk of cancer and are also thought to prevent cancer cells from multiplying if you are already suffering from the disease. Saponins are also believed to stimulate the immune system and reduce high cholesterol levels.

So, in a nutshell (or pod)

Legumes are fabulously healthy things to eat. We are constantly being advised to eat more food from plant rather than animal sources. A helping of pulses counts as one of the recommended five-a-day fruits and vegetables we should all be consuming. They're filling, will stop you snacking, and can help to prevent obesity, type 2 diabetes, heart disease and cancer.

All You Need to Know

How to Buy: Canned or Dried?

The great thing with legumes is that you have a tremendous amount of choice, not just in the varieties available but also in the time and energy that you're prepared to spend on them. Dried and canned pulses are fabulous storecupboard options as they keep for months and are among the most versatile ingredients in the kitchen.

Canned

My cupboard is always stocked with a selection of canned beans and chickpeas. They really are the ultimate convenience food. Before you buy, check that there's no added salt or sugar; there really doesn't need to be anything but pulse and water. Some cans may contain antioxidants such as metabisulphite or firming agents like calcium chloride; avoid these if possible. You will need to rinse the beans to get rid of the rather claggy water. If you are using chickpeas, you could set the liquid, known as aquafaba, aside to whip up for egg-free meringue, mousse, baked goods or frosting.

Canned pulses taste great, are highly nutritious and will undoubtedly save you time and energy. The downside is that a good-quality canned pulse will cost up to four times the equivalent home-cooked dried pulse by weight. But if you're catering for one, you could argue that all the power used during the prolonged cooking will offset the saving.

While I'll happily buy canned chickpeas and beans, lentils are another story. Dried lentils require no soaking, cook in about half an hour, have a much better texture and flavour when home-cooked and cost half the price. Need I say more? For similar reasons, I rarely buy canned mung, adzuki or black-eyed peas, but they do take longer to cook than lentils.

Dried

There's something rather meditative about dipping your hand into a sack of dried beans and letting them cascade through your fingers. Pulses should feel relatively heavy (a light bean could be last year's or, worse still, a weevil-infested hollow shell). Uniform size and colour are sought out too. The skins should be taut with no sign of a wrinkle. When inspecting a bean, the hilum (in effect its little navel but often referred to as an eye) should be bright and never show any brown or yellow discoloration.

For most of us, this careful selection process is irrelevant; we simply pick up a bag from the local supermarket. Recently supermarkets have given much more thought, time and shelf space to legumes, in response to more widely recognized need for healthier eating, and I'm pleased to say that the quality and range of beans on offer has generally improved too. I no longer seem to come across beans that take a lifetime to cook (a sure sign of a 'has been' that's spent too long in a warehouse). The other advantage of supermarket pulses is that they have been well cleaned and sorted, so you're less likely to come across an unwelcome pebble. My local health food shop has a fabulous range of organic legumes and advice on sprouting, cooking and combining.

A trip to a specialist Spanish, Italian, Middle Eastern, Indian or other ethnic store is a great way to source exciting and very good-quality legumes. Once you've tasted a *blanco lechoso* chickpea from Spain or an Italian Castelluccio lentil, you'll realize that there are some real treats to be had.

Dried pulses can be incredibly good value: a bag of beans doubles in weight, at the very least, once cooked. But you do need a plan: legumes really only work for the budget-conscious cook if you prepare larger quantities. The idea is to get in the habit of boiling up a decent-sized pot of beans and using them over a few days in various different recipes or even bunging a few in the freezer.

To Soak or Not to Soak?

It is entirely possible to cook pulses without any soaking at all. In Mexico, arguably the epicentre of world bean appreciation, there's no tradition of soaking the beans. Pulses just go in the pot with, or without, a few aromatics and perhaps a bit of fat and there they bubble away until tender and toothsome. So why not do the same?

Well, for one thing, dried pulses can take hours and hours to cook – depending on both their age and variety. The Mexican market does a brisk trade in beans, so while their beans are probably in their prime many of ours are likely to be distinctly older and will take an absolute age to cook if they're not soaked first.

While legumes require no attention at all during their overnight soak, a bubbling pot does demand a bit of hovering about. I want to keep the cooking to a minimum to save both energy and my time. A soaked bean cooks through more evenly, allowing the centre to become creamy and soft before the skin and outer flesh begin to collapse.

Finally, and most importantly, soaking is believed to improve our ability to absorb the wide range of nutrients found in beans. Washing away some of the phytic acid and the wind-inducing oligosaccharides makes the pulses more digestible whilst reducing any flatulent effects too. There are two main ways to soak your beans:

The overnight soak

This is the way to get the most smooth-textured, evenly cooked beans. Place your beans in a large bowl with about double their volume of water. Leave to soak overnight at room temperature (unless it's very warm, in which case they'll need to go into the refrigerator or another cool place, otherwise they can ferment). Drain before cooking.

The quick soak

I think of this as the 'resort to' option when you've forgotten to get ahead or you've just decided what to cook. It seems to me to require a bit more faff. Place the beans in a large pan and cover with plenty of water. Bring the water up to the boil and then remove from the heat and leave the beans soaking in the hot water for an hour. Drain the beans.

Soaking and cooking times

The table below gives optimum soaking times and approximate cooking times. These may vary in individual recipes. It's not essential but I do give smaller beans a short soak as it cuts down the cooking time and seems to result in fewer split skins and more evenly cooked results.

No Soak	Optional short soak: 2–3 hours	Recommended short soak: 2–3 hours	Long soak: at least 4 hours	Long soak: at least 8 hours or overnight
Lentils, split peas, split beans (often known as dal), moth beans, mung beans	Adzuki beans, black-eyed peas	Chana dal (split chickpeas), pigeon peas	All the New World beans: butter beans, lima beans, haricots, flageolets, kidney beans, black beans, borlotti, cannellini and pinto beans	Peas, fava beans, chickpeas, soya beans
Usually cook in 30–45 minutes	Usually cook in 30–45 minutes	Usually cook in under 1 hour	Usually cook in 1–2 hours	Usually cook in 1½–3 hours
				A pressure cooker will cut the cooking time. Or perhaps add a pinch of bicarbonate of soda (see page 19)

Cooking from Scratch

Why bother cooking your own legumes rather than simply opening a can? It's not just about saving money, or being able to track down some of the more highly prized and elusive varieties. When you prepare your own pulses, you can ensure they reach the perfect creamy texture, as well as enhancing their flavour with herbs, vegetables, bones and fats. There's the added bonus of the cooking liquid, too; this wonderful stock provides the base of many soups and stews. So don't tip your bean water down the sink – it's full of nutrients and flavour.

Cooking dried pulses requires nothing more than a bit of patience and a large pan. There are a few very general rules to follow.

Cover the pulses (soaked if necessary, see page 17) by just a few centimetres (an inch) of water, otherwise you will leach away much of the goodness. Colour, flavour and valuable nutrients are lost if you use too much cooking water. You will need to keep an eye on the beans as they cook and add a splash more water from time to time as required (just enough to keep the beans covered). Spanish cooks swear by adding chilled water to 'shock' the beans, helping them retain their skins, while in Mexico scalding hot water is the answer. My advice is not to get caught up in all the bean dogma. Cooking perfect beans really isn't rocket science.

Begin by boiling your beans for about 5 minutes. Red kidney beans require 10 minutes of boiling, to ensure that their high levels of toxins are deactivated (see page 38–39).

Reduce the heat to a very low simmer: too much turbulence and you'll lose the skins and end up with a mushy mess. Cover the pan with a lid and check occasionally that you have enough water. The simmer can take anything from 30 minutes to 3 hours or more, depending on the size, variety and age of your pulses. In general, the no-soakers take about half an hour, the quick-soakers under an hour and many of the long-soakers under two (see page 17). Your beans should, in true 007 style, be shaken but not stirred from time to time to ensure that they are not sticking (stirring will break them up).

Salt Adding salt to the water is reputed to toughen the skins and lengthen the cooking time, although nowadays many scientists are making the opposite claim. I stick with tradition as I find that early salting can give a mealy texture to the pulses. So, season the beans once cooked; it's easier to gauge how much salt to add at this stage. Pulses do cry out for seasoning otherwise they can taste bland, so I usually add at least 1 teaspoon of salt to 1kg/about 2lb cooked beans.

Bicarbonate of soda Many cooks suggest adding bicarbonate of soda to the cooking water, especially if you live in an area with particularly hard water (with high concentrations of minerals). There's no doubt that the skins do soften more quickly and the whole cooking process is speeded up, but at what cost? You will reduce the nutritional value of the beans considerably and sometimes end up with a rather soapy flavour. I only resort to baking soda with marrowfat peas and fava beans, which can take a lifetime to cook otherwise.

Acids and sugars These will stop the beans softening quickly, so tomatoes, molasses, wine and other sweet or sharp ingredients should usually be added only after the beans have cooked. This can be used to your advantage when you want to add cooked beans to casseroles and bakes without them collapsing.

Are they cooked?
A cooked bean should remain intact but the flesh will collapse into a creamy pulp when you squash it in your fingers; if there is a slight granular texture, it needs more cooking. Chickpeas will hold their shape even if they lose their skins, but do check that they are slightly creamy when squashed and have lost their starchy centre. Split lentils will collapse to a velvety purée, larger lentils will become soft and lack definition, while smaller lentils will hold their shape but should squash between your fingers or they will be mealy.

Sprouting

Until recently, the only sprouted bean you were likely to find outside specialist health food shops was the bean sprout (a sprouted mung bean) in your Chinese stir-fry. The myriad of other fabulous sprouts such as peas, chickpeas, lentils and peanuts were considered the domain of the earthy folk.

I have to admit, a few years ago I'd have been as likely to take up macramé as sprout my own legumes. But why not? As children we all witnessed the wonders of nature with a tray of cress on the school window sill. Sprouting is like an instant vegetable patch. It's so easy, cheap and ridiculously exciting. All you need is a large jar. You don't need to clutter your kitchen with trays of stagnating, damp cotton wool or to invest in a smart, tiered sprouter (although I do have one, and find it great when I'm after a bumper crop).

Many nutritionists believe that consuming raw, living food leads to better digestion, higher energy levels and even rejuvenation (oh, yes please). Once sprouted, a seed has far higher levels of vitamins, proteins and minerals than in its dormant state. So those little sprouts that look and taste so good have entered the realms of the 'superfood'.

Sprouts of all kinds are magic sprinkled on top of almost any salad, adding amazing texture and flavour. In fact, they are one of the few salad ingredients that my six-year-old daughter actually seems to relish. Try adding a handful into a sandwich or a stir-fry too.

How to sprout

The simplest way to sprout is in a glass jar; I use a Kilner jar, which come in various sizes. Soak your pulses, nuts or seeds in the jar, in plenty of cool water, for a few hours. This is when the seed comes back to life. The sprouts need to breathe, so secure a piece of muslin (cheesecloth) with an elastic band over the top of the jar. (I've read that some people

use micromesh tights, but that really doesn't appeal to me.) Carefully tip the water out through the muslin and allow the pulses to spread out along the length of the jar.

Leave the jar at an angle to continue draining onto a tray (this is where the lid of a Kilner jar forms a perfect stand). Place the jar somewhere at room temperature, out of direct sunlight. Now all you need to do, leaving the muslin in place, is fill the jar with cool water, give it a swirl and drain your beans at 12-hourly intervals until they have sprouted.

Once the sprout is as long as the seed, it's time to tuck in, but you can leave it to grow longer if you prefer. Sprouting times will vary according to the age of your seeds and room temperature, see guide on page 23.

To store the sprouts, give them a good final rinse and then let them drain. They need to be quite dry if you are storing them for more than a day in the refrigerator, so use a salad spinner or drain them on paper towels. Most sprouts will keep in the refrigerator for at least a week in a sealed container or resealable plastic bag. Sprouted chickpeas and peas, however, lose their crisp texture and are best eaten within 2 days.

Avoiding hiccups

The joy of sprouting is that it's very straightforward and you're not going to wake up to discover that an army of slugs has devastated your crop. However, there are a few things to keep in mind:

- Sprouts need to be well rinsed, drained and able to breathe, otherwise mould may develop.
- Wash the jar or sprouter thoroughly between crops. It's a good idea to sterilize it from time to time.
- Don't overpack the jar: the seeds should lie in a layer no more than two deep.
- Get your pulses from a reputable source (I always use organic for sprouting), and don't even think of using garden seeds, which might have been treated with chemicals.
- As with many raw foods, there is a small risk of food poisoning attached to eating sprouted pulses. Vulnerable groups such as infants, the elderly, those with compromised immune systems or pregnant women should avoid eating raw sprouted pulses, but can cook them thoroughly instead.

What to sprout

A pulse, just like a nut, is a dormant seed. It does seem bizarre to think of all those bags of dried beans, chickpeas and lentils in the supermarkets as bags of seeds just waiting to burst into life, but that's exactly what they are. Given moisture, air and the right temperature, they will miraculously sprout. Many health food shops and online suppliers sell you seeds that are perfect for sprouting, although when it comes to mainstream lentils and chickpeas, I just use what I have. **Ignore butter beans, kidney beans, haricots, flageolets, borlotti, cannellini and pinto beans, which have potentially serious allergy/ toxicity/digestibility issues.**

Bean	Soaking	Sprouting	Characteristics
Alfalfa	4 hours	3–4 days	Yes, it is a legume! The superfood hero, bursting with vitamins and minerals.
Adzuki beans	8–12 hours	3–4 days	Gorgeous bright colour, sweet nutty flavour.
Moth beans	8–12 hours	12–24 hours	Super quick, very tasty; the beginner's sprout.
Mung beans	8–12 hours	3–4 days	The ubiquitous bean sprout, but so much more exciting when eaten as a very fresh, immature sprout.
Chickpeas	12–14 hours	2–3 days	Great in salads, or use the sprouts for a different take on hummus and felafel.
Lentils	8–12 hours	1–2 days	Perhaps my favourite of the lot. The lentils must be intact (not split such as red lentils). Smaller lentils seem to be quicker off the mark. All varieties add a nutty, earthy flavour to salads, snacks and sandwiches and could be thrown into a stir-fry.
Peas	12–14 hours	2–3 days	Sweet like baby peas straight from the pod, children love them. I prefer green peas; yellow ones have a stronger flavour, and of course split peas won't work at all.
Peanuts	12–14 hours	2–4 days	Peanuts are botanically legumes and not nuts. Sprouts are best eaten when the peanut has just started to germinate, with a large bulge rather than an actual sprout at its tip (when they can taste bitter).

Check Your Pulse: The Identification Parade

Pulses are the edible seeds of plants from the Leguminosae family, such as beans, peas and lentils. These seeds all grow in pods (the fruit of the plant) and in some cases the pods are eaten too. Many pulses or legumes are commonly eaten fresh, such as peas and broad beans; some – such as the Italian borlotti – are left on the plant to semi-dry, but most are fully dried.

The selection of pulses on offer in supermarkets has grown considerably in recent years, health food shops often have a huge choice of shiny beans just waiting to be scooped up, and in some Asian and other ethnic shops the variety can be overwhelming.

There are simply thousands of varieties of pulse, or legume, grown around the world. Heirloom varieties are increasingly popular among gardeners but rarely available to buy. It did make me giggle as I perused the seed catalogues: in Britain we have distinctly unglamorous bean names such as 'Lazy Housewife' and 'District Nurse', while the North Americans are growing the evocative-sounding 'Black Calypso' and 'Red Nightfall' beans. I'll leave the allotment growers to their endless discussions over the differences between a black cow pea and a purple hull. People do seem to get hot under the collar about the ignorance of calling an adzuki a red cow pea, or the great conundrum of whether the mung bean should in fact be referred to as a pea. I had to detangle entire internet forums to come up with the somewhat simplified guide that follows.

These are the legumes that you are most likely to come across. Some may require a bit of tracking down, but most are widely available.

BEANS

Chickpea, garbanzo bean (*Cicer arietinum*)

Chickpeas are a native of the arid Middle East and have been cultivated for about 9,000 years. They are a staple food in a band of countries stretching from North Africa through the Levant to East India. Chickpeas were embraced by the ancient Greeks and Romans and later the Spanish (after they were introduced by the Moors) and now chickpeas are cooked all around the Mediterranean. The Iberians took them to the New World, but they've never begun to compete in popularity with the indigenous beans in the Americas, or in the Far East for that matter.

Chickpeas can be eaten fresh: they taste like a cross between an edamame and a fresh pea. I've only found them once or twice in Britain, but in the Middle East at harvest time they are snapped up for salads. The Californians are developing a taste for them too.

Desi chickpea, brown chickpea, Bengal gram, kala chana, black chickpea

Desi is the most common type of chickpea grown in Asia and is the closest relation of the wild chickpea. The tiny brown desi chickpea has a tough skin, a nutty, earthy flavour and is higher in fibre than its cousin the Kabuli. In India, this is the most widely used of all the legume family, and this is the variety you'll find in many traditional Asian curries. You'll probably find desi chickpeas only in Asian shops, but you can always substitute the readily available Kabuli chickpea.

Chana dal, daria dal

Chana dal are skinned and split Bengal gram used to make wonderfully creamy dals, a staple of vegetarian India. Remember to soak them for 2–3 hours otherwise they take an age to cook. Nowadays, we tend to associate chana dal primarily with the Indian subcontinent, but they have been found in ancient Egyptian tombs with the mummies – a quick snack for the afterlife. Roasted chana dal are known as daria dal, a popular ingredient in Indian chutneys and snacks.

Chickpea flour, gram flour, besan

This is ground from the skinned and split chickpeas. It's used widely in India for fried snacks such as pakoras, bhajia and poppadams. In the Mediterranean, the flour is traditionally made into roasted flatbreads called *socca* or *farinata*, as well as deep-fried nibbles. It's a fabulous ingredient for those on gluten-free diets. You will find it in health food shops, some supermarkets and Middle Eastern and Asian stores.

Kabuli chickpea

This is the type most of us are familiar with; it is grown in Europe and the Middle East. The chickpeas are pale beige with a wonderfully nutty flavour. There are dozens of varieties of Kabuli chickpeas. The huge *garbanzo lechoso*, or *blanco lechoso*, from Spain is one of my favourites, which I seek out from delis or Spanish suppliers for a special treat. The jars of cooked Spanish chickpeas are fabulous, too; they have such a creamy texture and make the best hummus imaginable (if you're not on a budget). Making your own hummus takes just a few minutes in a food processor, it's delicious, it's cheap, you know what's in it: it makes sense.

Chickpeas need a long soak and may take up to 4 hours of simmering to become tender. The upside is that, unlike beans, they won't collapse to a mush. It's always worth cooking a large batch, which you can use in several different ways or even freeze some. Canned chickpeas are a useful standby and I use them more than any other legume.

Broad bean, fava bean (*Vicia faba*)

The Old World's original bean, the fava, was an Egyptian staple back in the days of the pharaohs, although it was considered fit only for slaves and animals. The fava was the only bean known to Europeans for millennia but it did not always enjoy great popularity. The Greeks believed that any wind experienced as a result of eating the beans was the souls of the dead passing from their resting place in the ground, through the soil, into the bean and finally through your body. Now there's a thought next time you suffer from a little flatulence.

Broad beans were associated with death and burials by the Romans and Celts too. All these morbid connections are perhaps no coincidence, since there is a potentially fatal syndrome connected with eating fava beans. Favism is a rare condition that strikes people with a particular enzyme deficiency, many of whom live in, or can trace their origins back to, the southern Mediterranean or the Middle East.

Dried fava beans

Dried broad beans or fava beans, known as 'ful', are consumed in huge quantities across the Eastern Mediterranean, Middle East and the Horn of Africa. Surprisingly, huge quantities of the beans are grown in East Anglia, dried and then shipped to the Arab world. So, rather ironically since they are one of Britain's only homegrown dried pulses, they are not easy to track down in British supermarkets, although Greek, Turkish or Middle Eastern shops will certainly stock them.

The whole, dried brown beans are typically used in the Egyptian national dish of *ful medames*, but you will find variations on the size and type of fava bean used all around the Levant.

The slightly bitter flavour of broad beans (from the tannins in their skin) can be an acquired taste. Remove some of the bitterness by tipping away the soaking water and also by changing the cooking water after about 20 minutes. Favas do take a long time to soften, so be patient, add a teaspoon of bicarbonate of soda to the cooking water or, better still, use a pressure cooker. Quicker cooking, shelled and split fava beans are better suited to making felafel (the Egyptians use fava beans rather than chickpeas) and purées rather similar to hummus.

Adzuki, aduki, azuki, red chouri (*Vigna angularis*)

Was it the Japanese, the Koreans or the Chinese who first cultivated these tiny maroon-red beans? It's a hotly contested issue, so let's just call the adzuki an East Asian bean.

The idea of sweet beans may seem strange to most of us in the West, but in the Far East most adzuki are traditionally cooked with sugar and made into the red bean paste that is used in many desserts and sweets, such as mooncakes, dumplings and ice cream.

The adzuki bean is fabulous in savoury dishes too. The cooked beans are sometimes stir-fried in China. In India, where they are often known as red chouri, they end up in dals and curries. The adzuki is also a big player in some parts of Africa: in Somalia, it is mixed with butter and sugar in the sweet dish *cambuulo*.

Adzuki beans cook in about 40 minutes from dry and even more quickly if you get around to soaking them. Their nutty flavour is wonderful in salads, stir-fries and curries, and they're also one of my favourite beans to sprout.

Mung bean, green/golden gram, moong dal (*Vigna radiata*)

The chameleon of beans, the mung bean pops up in different guises around the world. We've all been eating mung beans for years, perhaps without even knowing it. Back in my student days, it was only the crisp white bean sprouts and a dash of soy sauce that lent those rather dubious stir-fries a touch of the exotic. In China, the mung bean is eaten mostly as a bean sprout but also, in common with most of East Asia, sweetened with sugar and served as a dessert.

Another mung bean incarnation is the cellophane or glass noodle made from mung bean starch. These spectacularly light noodles are fabulous in soups, broths and salads, soaking up flavours and adding their wispy body to a dish.

In the Arab world mung beans are often prepared with rice and spices or cooked in vegetable casseroles. The beans require no soaking and are usually ready in about 45 minutes, so they make a great storecupboard standby.

In Indian cuisine, the mung bean becomes completely unrecognizable. Moong dal (aka green gram or golden gram) is skinned and split, revealing the golden interior often confused with a lentil. The split beans break down into the most fabulously creamy texture for delicious dals.

Moth bean, mat/matki bean, dew bean, Turkish gram (*Vigna aconitifolia*)

You are not going to find moth beans (pronounced 'moat' ... sound a bit more appetizing?) in your local corner shop unless you live somewhere with a large Indian community. However, as a keen sprouter, I just couldn't leave them out. These rather unassuming-looking little beans burst into crunchy sprouts in about 24 hours and then make the most fabulous stir-fry ingredient.

Moth beans make good substitutes for mung beans and can be cooked from dry in about 20 minutes.

Urad dal, urd, black gram, kali dal (*Vigna mungo*)

You will probably only find tiny urd or urad beans in specialist Indian shops or online. They are highly prized in their homeland, where they are considered to make the very best dals and have religious significance to the Hindus. The tiny black beans are sometimes confused with black lentils, but on close inspection they are quite obviously beans.

They are sometimes cooked whole, but more often than not they are skinned and split, revealing their white interiors (unlike the mung bean which is more golden). The dry split beans are often quick-fried, almost like a spice, to add texture and flavour to various pickles. The flour ground from the split beans is used in all sorts of southern Indian specialities such as pappads, idli and poppadams.

Cow pea, black-eyed pea, lobhia
(*Vigna unguiculata*)

Let's start by pointing out that it's not a pea at all; scientifically speaking, it's a bean, but as far as the cook's concerned, does it really matter? Not all cow peas have the distinctive black marking of the black-eyed pea, but it is the most common variety.

The cow pea originated in Africa and is still one of the most important sub-Saharan crops. The plants are incredibly hardy and can withstand extremely hot, dry conditions and grow in poor sandy soils. Cow peas were grown in ancient Greece (they're still a Greek favourite) and Rome and quickly spread throughout Asia, turning up in Indian dals and as fresh yard-long beans in China and the Far East.

Black-eyed peas are hugely popular in the southern United States (and I'm not talking hip-hop now), where they are cooked up with pork and rice for the traditional New Year's dish of Hoppin' John. Many mistakenly assume that they're an American native, but in fact the black-eyed peas made their way over to America, Brazil and the Caribbean with African slaves. Not just the beans, but traditional dishes came too. *Acarajé*, the deep-fried dried shrimp and black-eyed pea cakes sold on the streets of Brazilian Bahia, are closely related to Nigerian *akara*.

These little beans cook in less than an hour, and you can halve the time if you remember to soak them. They are fabulous in salads, rice dishes and stews, with their earthy, almost minerally flavour.

Pigeon pea, gungo pea, Congo pea/bean, gandule bean, toor/tuvar/toovar dal (*Cajanus cajan*)

Another bean posing as a pea. Pigeon peas are probably most familiar in the Caribbean dish of rice and peas. They are also a vital crop in Africa (they arrived in the Americas with the slave trade), where as well as using them dried, they are often eaten fresh: shoots, leaves and all.

Pigeon peas are also immensely popular in India. You are most likely to find them skinned and split as toor dal, used to make the nutritious porridgey soups known as dal. Toor dal can be confused with split yellow peas or chana dal (split chickpeas): while they may have rather different textures, flavours (toor are quite gelatinous and very savoury) and cooking times, you could get away with substituting one for another.

You may also come across oily toor dal, which have been treated with vegetable oil to prolong their shelf life. You need to give them a good rinse before cooking.

Black beans (fermented)

Chinese fermented and salted soya beans (see overleaf) are usually referred to simply as black beans. They have no connection with the Mexican black (turtle) bean. The pungent little beans are used as a seasoning in sauces and stir-fries, giving an amazing range of bitter, sweet, sour, salty flavour.

You can buy the beans by the bag from Asian stores. Once opened, they will keep for several months in an airtight container. It's an idea to rinse the beans before use, as they can be very salty. Black bean paste or sauce is available in many supermarkets too.

Soya bean, soybean (*Glycine max*)

This Old World bean is relatively new to the West, but has achieved global dominance in the past 80 years. The Jekyll and Hyde of the bean world, soya is by far and away the most widely produced and consumed pulse on the planet; it is also both the most celebrated and the most controversial. Soy has been a food crop for over 5,000 years; originally considered the food of the poor in ancient China, it is now one of the mainstays of industrial food production throughout the world.

The soya bean is streets ahead of all the other pulses in its oil content (about 20%) and protein content (about 40%). It is, unlike other pulses, considered a 'complete' protein capable of providing all the essential amino acids, and is thus a great alternative to animal protein.

Edamame (green soya beans)

Edamame are fresh or frozen, green, immature soya beans that are sold in the pod or ready podded. Blanched quickly, they make a delicious snack served with a pinch of salt. The fabulous lime-green colour of the beans will lift all sorts of bean salads and stir-fries, and they are a low-fat, high-protein addition to any healthy meal.

Tofu or bean curd

Tofu could be called the cheese of the East. Soy milk, extracted from the cooked beans, is curdled by adding either salty or acid coagulants, and the curd is then pressed into cakes. Try to buy organic tofu and prepare it yourself rather than buying highly processed tofu products. It is best to drain firm tofu before use. Silken tofu has a much softer, creamier texture and is often prepared as an uncooked savoury dish, dessert or dairy-free sauce. Tofu on its own is incredibly bland, but given the right treatment can be absolutely delicious.

Tempeh

Tempeh bears little resemblance to the neutral blank canvas that is tofu: it has a distinctive and delicious savoury flavour of its own. Like tofu, tempeh is a bean curd, but it is fermented in an ancient process that originated in Indonesia. You will probably find tempeh in a vacuum pack in your local health store; it won't look like much but I do urge you to give it a go. Fried up and served with a splash of chilli sauce, it might even convert the resolute carnivore.

Miso

Miso is a fermented paste that lends an amazingly nutty, salty and savoury depth wherever you use it. The paste is usually made with soya beans, salt, rice or barley and a fungus, or starter culture and ranges from mild-tasting pale, creamy-coloured miso to dark miso with a more mature, stronger flavour. It's a staple of the Japanese kitchen but is used in much of East Asia.

Soy sauce

The traditional Chinese and Japanese condiment has become a universal ingredient. It is traditionally made by fermenting a mixture of soya beans, wheat and salt with various types of bacteria and yeast, over several months. There are many inferior soy sauces made by a much speedier process and so I always look for those labelled 'organic' or 'naturally brewed'.

As with miso paste, when dealing with the naturally fermented sauces, the darker the sauce, the more pronounced the flavour. Tamari, one of my favourite soy sauces, is a traditional Japanese sauce made without wheat. Ketjap manis, the Indonesian soy, is syrupy, sweetened with sugar and flavoured with spices.

Butter bean, lima bean, Madagascar bean (*Phaseolus lunatus*)

The butter bean is a bean apart from all the other Latino beans, not just because of its size and creamy texture but also because of its Andean origins. It is from a quite different bean family from all the kidney and haricot beans, and many would say a more aristocratic bean altogether.

Butter beans are perhaps my number one bean; they're wonderful in salads and work well with mustardy vinaigrettes, they have an affinity with leeks and are fabulous with creamy or more acidic tomato sauces. However, they can be quite a challenge to cook. They require a long overnight soak and then a really slow, gentle simmer, otherwise they seem to shed their skins and collapse more readily than other beans.

The Spanish *judiones* are my favourite variety, and I quite often cheat by using the jars of ready-cooked creamy beans. They are an extravagance, but worth every penny – you can really understand why they are called 'butter' beans.

The dried Greek *gigantes* ('giant' or 'elephant') beans are spectacular, although most supermarkets seem to sell them ready-cooked in a tomato sauce.

Definitions get complicated in North America, where many varieties of lima beans are grown and eaten fresh as well as dried. In the southern US, the term 'butterbean' refers to the smaller, flat green beans instead of the large, slippery, creamy variety we are talking about.

Almost all of the *Phaseolus lunatus* family need cooking, be they fresh or dried, as they contain varying levels of cyanide. Commercial varieties have been selected for their safer, lower levels, but should you start growing your own, it's probably best to cut out any garden grazing. For more details, I recommend the joyfully named tome, *How To Poison Your Spouse the Natural Way* by Jay D. Mann.

Borlotti, coco rose, Roman bean, cranberry bean (*Phaseolus vulgaris*)

If there was ever a bean to make a fashion statement, it would be the borlotti, with its pink Missoni-style jacket. The fresh pods are a stunning sight in summer markets. The magic continues as you open the pods to reveal the beans within, each speckled like an exquisite little wren's egg. The most readily available beans are dried, but do try to track down the fresh beans if you can. These require no soaking, will cook in about 30 minutes, and are fabulous smothered in extra-virgin olive oil.

The celebrity of the borlotti world is, without a doubt, the Lamon bean from the Italian Alps. All the borlotti, coco rose, Roman and cranberry beans are closely related and probably evolved from the Colombian *cargamonto* bean. I happily interchange them and tend to use the most evocative name to suit the menu or the dish. Once cooked, the beans do lose their rather chichi markings, turning a deep reddish brown, but what they lose in looks they more than make up for in creamy flavour.

Flageolet bean (*Phaseolus vulgaris*)

These little green celebrities of the French bean world are also known as chevrier verts, in honour of Monsieur Gabriel Chevrier who first cultivated them in the 1870s outside Paris. It's a particular strain of dwarf haricot that retains its fresh green colour due to its ability to retain chlorophyll, even once dried in the pod. And, unlike so many beans that lose their glamour in the pot, the flageolet is a stunner once cooked too and has a fine skin that makes it easily digestible and especially creamy. It works wonderfully with lamb, pork, cream and tarragon.

Another variety of small green bean that is worth a mention is the Spanish *verdina* bean. With a lustrous jade-green skin, this is the ultimate bean to prepare with clams, as they do in Asturias. The north coast of Spain is a bean Mecca and well worth a visit.

Cannellini bean (*Phaseolus vulgaris*)

One of the most famous Italian beans is the cannellini. It's a white kidney bean, possibly an Argentinian native, that has made itself at home in central and southern Italy.

You may be lucky enough to find fresh cannellini in their pods, as they are sometimes sold in Italy. They are allowed to mature fully on the plant, so they will need plenty of cooking (about half an hour or so), and you will lose about half their weight in the pods, but they are heaven. Dried beans are the more likely prospect. Cannellini are particularly creamy and slightly nutty-tasting and lend themselves beautifully to vegetable soups and salads doused in extra-virgin olive oil.

As a close relation of the red kidney bean, it's a good precaution to boil these for 10 minutes at the beginning of the cooking to avoid any possibility of food poisoning (see red kidney beans below).

Another highly fêted white kidney bean is the Spanish *faba de Asturias*, the star ingredient in the local pork and bean dish, but its production is limited and price usually exorbitant.

Red kidney bean, rajma dal (*Phaseolus vulgaris*)

The ubiquitous bean of chilli con carne. Yet kidney beans have so much more to offer: they look fantastic, have a firm texture, hold together well and have a slightly sweet, almost meaty flavour. They are fabulous paired with sharp and hot, spicy flavours. Red kidney beans are particularly popular in Latin American, Caribbean and Indian cooking, where they are often teamed up with rice.

Plenty of people are rather cautious about cooking beans from scratch and it's the red kidney we have to blame. Many of the common beans contain a toxin called phytohaemagglutinin, but it's only the red kidney bean that contains high enough concentrations to cause real problems, which can range from an upset stomach to full-on food poisoning. A good long soak and a change of water before cooking are advisable, but the crucial bit is the boiling. The toxin is deactivated by boiling for 10 minutes, so the long, slow simmer required to soften the beans should always be preceded by the boil. Slow cookers are fine as long as you remember to boil for 10 minutes first, otherwise you will actually be increasing the toxin levels.

Haricot bean, navy bean, pea bean (*Phaseolus vulgaris*)

If you've only ever eaten one bean as a Brit, it will be this one! The British consume haricots by the ton in cans of good old baked beans. The tiny round haricot is rather bland, not something I would put into a salad, for example, but it soaks up other flavours such as tomatoes and pork wonderfully well. So the haricot is ideal for slow-cooked dishes such as the traditional Boston baked beans and that king of all bean pots, the cassoulet of south-west France.

There are many varieties of haricot that fit their own local dish perfectly, such as the Tarbais or white coco that star in cassoulet. White coco, and other varieties such as the Spanish *pochas*, are sometimes cooked semi-fresh, straight from the pod. The French *haricots de Soissons* are the giants of the common bean world and have the most velvety texture imaginable when puréed into soups. The American Great Northern bean is a larger type of haricot that works well in casseroles and stews, and is a popular substitute for the navy bean in traditional baked beans.

Meanwhile in Tuscany, the Italian bean capital, pale yellow *zolfino* and the pearly-white *sorana* beans attract gastronomic pilgrimages. Other white beans to look out for are the diminutive *arrocina*, or 'rice', beans from Spain, which I have found in my local deli. These creamy little beans have lots of flavour and hold their shape well.

Pinto bean (*Phaseolus vulgaris*)

Literally 'painted bean', named for their rather splotchy mottled skins, these are the most commonly used beans in north-west Mexico and the southern United States. The pinto more often than not ends up as the refried bean or piled into a chilli.

Other very similar but not so widely available beans are rattlesnake, appaloosa and anasazi beans. You'd probably have to be in cowboy country to track any of those down, but who knows? There's a huge resurgence of interest in heirloom beans in the US right now; give it a few years and I'll probably spot them on my local supermarket shelf. In the meantime, I'll raise a few eyebrows by suggesting a borlotti in its place. It may not have quite the same sweet beany flavour, and the skin is a little thicker, but by the time you've got all the Mexican trappings, will anybody notice?

The Basques have their own speckled *pinta alavesa* and the rather similar red a*lubia de Gernika* and maroon/black *alubia de Tolosa* bean. Oh I know that I'll be chastised for this by some Basque bean fancier or even the local bean brotherhood (and yes, there is one!), but these beans refry very well and are delicious cooked up with all manner of porky things and served with a touch of chilli heat – just like a pinto.

Black bean, black turtle bean (*Phaseolus vulgaris*)

Dramatic black beans turn to a glorious deep purple once cooked in their most traditional guise – *frijoles de la olla*, or pot beans. Growers can track down evocatively named varieties such as Zorro, Black Valentine and Nighthawk, but most of us will have to make do with the good old black turtle. They are all varieties of the same little Mexican bean, with its dense, meaty texture and sweet, almost mushroomy, flavour.

Black beans are a little firmer than the cooked pinto, so this is my bean of choice when I want to make a zippy salad or fling some beans into a spiced vegetable soup. Black beans are very popular in Latin America, where they are the stars of Brazilian *feijoada*, and right across the Caribbean. They have nothing to do with Asian fermented black beans (see page 33).

Bambara groundnut, bambara bean (*Vigna subterranea*) and peanut, groundnut, goober pea, monkey nut (*Arachis hypogaea*)

Peanuts and groundnuts are, scientifically speaking, legumes and not nuts. The bambara groundnut and the peanut are extremely unusual in that their edible seeds grow and ripen underground. There are many similarities between the two and yet they have totally different origins. The bambara groundnut is an African species and is widely cultivated in much of West Africa as it can withstand incredibly hot, dry growing conditions. These nuts provide vital protein for people living on marginal agricultural land.

The peanut came from South America and was introduced by the Europeans to Africa and to North America. The peanut is more productive and easier to harvest than the groundnut, and it's higher in protein and oil. Rather confusingly, it has become known as a groundnut as well.

Nowadays huge quantities of peanuts are grown in Asia, where they are used primarily for oil. In sub-Saharan Africa, groundnut stew (and this time we're talking peanuts) is a staple dish that provides vital protein, minerals, vitamins and calories to millions every day. Meanwhile, in the US and Europe, the peanut is consumed mostly as a snack or as peanut butter.

PEAS (*Pisum sativum*)

Peas are one of the ancient crops from the Fertile Crescent of the Middle East, which have been cultivated for around 9,000 years. They quickly spread across Europe and Asia and became a key source of protein in much of northern Europe. Peas are a winter crop in the Mediterranean basin, thriving in the cooler, damper weather, and so they are brilliantly suited to the northern climate.

Of all the pulses, dried peas seem to take the longest to cook. This is why split peas are so much better for soups than any of the whole dried peas. So, although in most cases I'm not a great fan of adding bicarbonate of soda to my pot (see page 19), when I use whole peas I sometimes make an exception, otherwise they could be bubbling all day before they soften. A pressure cooker can really speed things up.

Marrowfat peas

The only acceptable pea to use for Britain's traditional mushy peas. These are peas that have been left to plump up, mature and partially dry on the plant. They are then fully dried. When cooking, an alkaline such as bicarbonate of soda is useful to ensure soft, mushy results. You can buy marrowfats dried, canned, or already processed into mushy peas. I have to admit that I'd always turned my nose up at the canned peas until I came upon a quick trick from the fabulous Nigella. Just whizz up a drained can of peas with a ripe avocado, a clove or two of garlic and a dash of fresh lime juice. An instant crostini topping.

Carlin peas

Also known rather fabulously as black badger peas, red fox peas or maple peas, these old Northern English peas have been enjoying a bit of a come back of late. Traditionally served as 'parched peas' with nothing more than salt and vinegar, they are wonderfully nutty in flavour and work well in curries and salads.

Blue and yellow peas

Not that easy to come by, these peas take some time to cook but give wonderful results in spiced dishes. You could try sprouting them for a great burst of sweet flavour over the top of a salad. Rather confusingly, once a blue pea is skinned and split it becomes a split green pea!

Split peas

These are dried peas that have been skinned and split in half. Green and yellow split peas are interchangeable in any recipe. Green split peas have more of a 'pea-like' flavour. Yellow are the most traditional in all the old English and northern European classic soups and pottages, but there's nothing to stop you throwing in the green sort instead. Both make a fabulous backdrop for a hearty winter soup or play starring roles in many of the creamy dals of India.

Split peas are ideal for infants and anyone who finds pulses tricky to digest. There's no need to soak them either, although it will cut down the cooking time. Split peas can be substituted for red lentils but will take longer to cook.

LENTILS (*Lens culinaris*)

There are dozens of varieties of lentil around the world, so we will deal with the most common or readily available. To complicate matters further, many of the dals of southern Asia that are commonly considered lentils, such as *toor dal* or *urad dal*, are in fact split beans.

Lentils are wonderfully convenient: they require no soaking and cook in anything between 20–45 minutes. The key things to keep in mind are that tiny, whole lentils tend to hold together well, larger flatter lentils begin to soften and break down more quickly, and hulled split lentils will always be soft and mushy once cooked. So choose the lentil to suit your dish. The following small, whole lentils are all pretty interchangeable, although I'm sure some local chefs will be up in arms at this suggestion.

Puy lentil

The king of the castle, a marbled teal-green and slate-hued lentil from the volcanic soils of the Auvergne in France. This is the celebrity lentil with its own Appellation d'Origine Contrôlée, like a fine wine. Puy lentils have a wonderful nutty and almost peppery flavour.

Confession: I have also cheated with the Puy lookalikes, labelled small French lentils, with very acceptable results.

Castelluccio, or Umbrian, lentil

Italians love their lentils. They are traditionally served at New Year, each lentil representing a tiny coin that swells in the stock and promises a prosperous year ahead. The tiny greenish-brown Umbrian lentil, with its sweet, earthy flavour, grows on the Castelluccio plains and is sought out by chefs all over Europe. Like the Puy, it has its own protected geographical status.

Pardina lentil

The *lenteja pardina* is the Spanish tiny, hold-its-shape lentil. It doesn't look very glamorous (*pardo* translates as dull brown), but these are some of my favourite lentils to use. They have a nutty, almost herbaceous, flavour and they have their own protected status too.

Black beluga lentil

The glistening black North American lentil may look like caviar when it's raw, but it does lose a bit of its designer edge once cooked. I wouldn't bust a gut seeking these out over any of the other tiny lentils, but they are a very tasty option and do add a certain glitz to your menu.

Rustic lentils

The brown, or green, lentil is the common-or-garden lentil for soups, stews and mashes. It's bigger and flatter than its diminutive cousins (above). There are no flashy names or high price tags, but don't turn your nose up at the rustic flat lentil, it could be just what you're after. Sometimes you do want a lentil that will soften and break down into a creamy mash for a soup or stew. These softer lentils are perfect in Middle Eastern dishes or in a Spanish porky *cazuela*.

Split lentils: red lentils, Egyptian lentils, masoor dal

These are all very similar. They are hulled (skinned) and split lentils and so they cook more quickly, collapse to a mush and are more easily digested than whole lentils. Split lentils make fabulous soups and dals. With a bag of these in the cupboard, a cheap and nutritious dinner is never far away. Many other split pulses are used to make Indian dals, but these are actually split gram (beans or chickpeas) rather than lentils.

Nibbles & Dips

Cheat's creamy bean crostini

**Serves 4 as a starter,
or 20 as crostini**

400g/14oz can cannellini, haricot
(navy) or flageolet beans
2 garlic cloves, roughly chopped
4 tbsp olive oil
juice of ½ lemon
salt and pepper
crostini, to serve
a few leaves of parsley, basil or
marjoram (optional)
harissa, pesto, salsa verde or
romesco, to serve

For those in a hurry or with absolutely no inclination
to cook.

Whizz the beans, garlic, oil, lemon juice, salt and
pepper in a food processor or with a hand-held
blender. Taste the purée and adjust the seasoning.
The flavour of the creamed beans will be subtle but
needs to be balanced.

Put a tablespoon of purée on each crostini, pop on a
leaf or two of your chosen herb and then top with a
teaspoon of harissa, pesto, salsa verde or romesco
straight from the jar or home-made.

Green lentil tapenade

**Serves 4 as a starter,
8 as a dip**

A great combination that I stumbled upon in my kitchen one day – only to discover later that *elaiosalata* is a regular on the Greek meze table. Whereas the Greeks use their distinctive oregano, I prefer to add plenty of rosemary. Delicious served on crostini with roasted red peppers, mixed with some tinned tuna and spread on a sandwich, or as a stuffing for Spanish piquillo peppers.

150g/5½oz/¾ cup green lentils, rinsed

2 garlic cloves, crushed

1 large sprig of rosemary, stem removed and leaves finely chopped

3 tbsp capers, rinsed and drained

100g/3½oz/¾ cup pitted Kalamata olives

4 anchovy fillets in oil, drained

4 tbsp extra-virgin olive oil

juice of ½–1 lemon

salt and pepper

Put the lentils in a saucepan and cover with a good 10cm/4 inch of cold water. Bring to the boil and then simmer until tender; this may take anything from 20–45 minutes, depending on the lentils.

Drain and immediately (while the lentils are still warm) pulse together everything except the lemon juice and seasoning. I prefer to use a hand-held blender in the saucepan, keeping washing-up to a minimum, but you could put everything into a food processor or blender. Taste and add salt, pepper and lemon juice as required.

Southern Indian chickpeas and coconut

Serves 4

There are so many amazing Indian snacks made with pulses, but it was the pure simplicity of this recipe that caught my eye. It is traditionally served outside the temples of southern India during the Hindu festival of Navratri. Once eaten never forgotten, these chickpeas make a great little nibble to serve before a curry.

1 tbsp vegetable oil, such as rapeseed, sunflower, groundnut (peanut) or coconut oil

1 tsp black mustard seeds

1 green chilli, very finely diced

1 tsp very finely chopped fresh ginger

5 curry leaves (optional)

½ tsp salt

1 tbsp urad dal, or – very unorthodox – red lentils (optional)

250g/9oz home-cooked chickpeas (garbanzo beans), or 400g/14oz can chickpeas, rinsed

4 tbsp freshly grated coconut or 2 tbsp unsweetened desiccated (shredded) coconut

handful of fresh coriander (cilantro), finely chopped

Heat the vegetable oil in a large frying pan over a medium heat, add the mustard seeds and wait until they begin to splutter.

Throw in the chilli, ginger, curry leaves, salt and raw dal or lentils, if using. When the aromas burst out of the pan and the lentils begin to crisp up, then stir in the chickpeas. Remove from the heat and stir well. Add the coconut and coriander and dive in – scrumptious warm or cold.

Hummus

**Serves 4 as a starter,
8 as a dip**

This makes a welcome change from the more familiar *houmous bi tahini*. The slightly rougher texture of home-cooked chickpeas is preferable in this recipe.

300g/10½oz home-cooked chickpeas (garbanzo beans), or 400g/14oz can chickpeas, rinsed

2 garlic cloves, crushed

juice of 1 lemon

250ml/9fl oz/1 cup extra-virgin olive oil

salt and pepper

Place the chickpeas in a food processor with the garlic and lemon juice. Blend for a moment or two before adding most of the olive oil. Pulse the mixture, adding more oil as needed, until you have a nicely textured, rather than smooth, paste. Season to taste.

Try adding to the hummus: 2 tsp roasted and ground cumin seeds; 1 hot chilli, finely diced; or a handful of chopped fresh parsley or coriander (cilantro).

Red pepper hummus
2 roasted red peppers, peeled and deseeded, and 1 tsp smoked hot Spanish paprika, or cheat with Spanish piquillo peppers from a jar. Blend, add the hummus, above, and blend again to combine.

Roast pumpkin or carrot hummus
Preheat the oven to 200°C/400°F/gas mark 6. In a roasting pan, toss 600g/1lb 5oz peeled and roughly chopped pumpkin or carrot with 2 tbsp olive oil and 1 tsp cumin seeds. Roast for about 40 minutes, until the vegetables are very tender. Blend, add the hummus, above, and blend again to combine.

Roasted garlic hummus
Add 5 peeled garlic cloves to the roasting pan with the pumpkin or carrots (or red peppers, if you are roasting your own); remove once golden but not burned. Whizz with the roasted vegetables in a food processor until fairly smooth. Add the hummus, above, and whizz to combine. Taste and adjust the seasoning.

Syrian-style lentils

Serves 4 as a starter

Not strictly speaking a dip or purée, more of a mush really, but this humble dish is truly moreish and always seems more than the sum of its parts. It makes a great addition to any meze selection and is wonderful scooped up with flatbread for a light lunch or with rice for dinner.

4 tbsp olive oil

2 brown onions, finely sliced

6 garlic cloves, finely chopped

1 tsp cumin seeds, toasted and then ground

pinch of chilli flakes, or better still 2 tsp sweet Aleppo chilli flakes

200g/7oz/1 cup brown or green lentils, rinsed

salt and pepper

juice of ½–1 lemon

small bunch of coriander (cilantro), roughly chopped

Heat the oil in a large saucepan and add the onions. Keep the temperature fairly low and allow the onions to soften, sweeten and turn golden; this may take about 20 minutes. Be patient.

Take out half of the onions from the pan and set aside. Turn up the heat and throw in the garlic, cumin and chilli. Stir and, as soon as you can really smell the garlic, add the lentils and enough water to cover them by about 5cm/2 inches.

Bring to the boil and then turn down to a simmer. Cover the pan and cook until the lentils soften and begin to break down. You may have to add a little extra water from time to time if they are getting dry but go carefully; remember that you don't want to drain away any delicious juices later. Once the lentils are really soft, and this can take over an hour, taste and adjust the seasoning with salt, pepper and enough lemon juice to freshen the dish up. Stir in the coriander leaves and garnish with the remaining fried onions.

Serve with flatbread and perhaps a dollop of creamy Greek yogurt if you are feeling indulgent.

Sun-dried tomato, butterbean & pistachio pâté

250g/9oz/2 cups pistachios
2 tbsp olive oil
½ tsp sweet smoked paprika
pinch of salt
100g/3½oz sun-dried tomatoes
1 small red onion, diced
2 garlic cloves
1 large sprig of rosemary, leaves finely chopped
2 large sprigs of thyme, leaves finely chopped
1 tbsp balsamic vinegar
200g/7oz home-cooked butter beans (large lima beans), or 400g/14oz can butter beans, rinsed
small handful of fresh basil
50g/1¾oz/½ cup ground almonds

To serve:
sourdough toast
small jar of cornichons or gherkins
chutney or onion marmalade

Preheat the oven to 180°C/350°F/gas mark 4. Tip the pistachios onto a baking sheet, toss them in half the oil, the smoked paprika and a pinch of salt. Roast for 7 minutes (but check after 4 – this would be an expensive cremation calamity), until lightly roasted.

Put the sun-dried tomatoes in a small bowl, cover with boiling water and leave to soak.

Heat the remaining oil in a heavy pan and cook the onion over a low heat until soft. Throw in the garlic and herbs and season. Once the onion is caramelized, add the balsamic vinegar and stir over the heat for a minute or two. Drain the tomatoes and blitz in a food processor with the onion mixture, the butter beans and basil to make a rough purée. Remove and set aside.

Put about 50g/1¾oz/½ cup of the pistachios in the processor and pulse quickly to chop them coarsely. Throw them in with the bean mixture then blitz the remaining pistachios as finely as possible. Add the finely ground pistachios and the almonds to the bean purée and mix everything really thoroughly to combine. The pâté should seem really stiff. You can add a few more ground almonds if it seems too moist, keeping in mind that it will firm up a bit once chilled. Press the pâté into a terrine mould or loaf pan and chill for a couple of hours.

Serve with toast, cornichons, chutney or marmalade.

Black bean and chipotle dip

**Serves 4 as a starter,
8 as a dip**

2 tbsp olive oil

1 onion, finely diced

3 garlic cloves, finely diced

1 tsp ground cumin

250g/9oz home-cooked black beans, or 400g/14oz can black beans, rinsed

2 chipotle chillies in adobo sauce, stalks removed

2 tbsp sour cream, plus extra to serve

juice of 1–2 limes

salt

1 tbsp chopped fresh coriander (cilantro)

Tabasco sauce (optional)

Here's a Tex-Mex winner to serve alongside guacamole, tomato salsa and a few corn chips. Crack open an ice-cold beer, add a wedge of lime and let the fiesta begin.

Heat the oil in a pan and cook the onion gently until soft and golden. Add the garlic and cumin and continue to cook until it smells wonderful.

Put the onion mixture into a food processor with the beans and half of your chipotles (it's always wise to tread carefully with any chilli). Whizz to a purée and then add the remaining chilli, sour cream, lime juice and salt by degrees until the dip is balanced.

Stir in most of the coriander, check the seasoning again, and add a dash of Tabasco if you're feeling fiery. Serve with a swirl of sour cream and a sprinkling of coriander.

Small Bites

Beetroot and feta felafel

Makes about 16

True falafel are made with long-soaked, raw pulses and are then deep-fried whilst this unorthodox version makes a quicker, healthier option for the home cook.

450g/1lb beetroot (beets), washed and leaves trimmed

3 tbsp olive oil

250g/9oz home-cooked chickpeas (garbanzo beans), or 400g/14oz can chickpeas, rinsed

100g/3½oz feta cheese

2 garlic cloves, crushed

1 tsp cumin seeds, roasted and ground

large pinch of cayenne pepper

½ tsp salt

2 tbsp roughly chopped parsley

juice of ½–1 lemon

4 spring onions (scallions), finely sliced

Preheat the oven to 200°C/400°F/gas mark 6.

Leave the beetroot whole, drizzle with 1 tablespoon of the olive oil and wrap in a foil parcel. Roast until a knife glides into the flesh easily: this could take anything between 30 minutes and 1 hour, depending on the size and freshness of the beetroot. Leave to cool and then peel; the skin should just slip off.

Blitz the beetroot in a food processor with two-thirds of the chickpeas, the feta cheese, garlic, cumin, cayenne pepper, salt, parsley and lemon juice. Scrape the mixture into a mixing bowl and stir in the spring onions and the remaining chickpeas.

Chill the mixture for an hour if you can (it makes it easier to handle), before shaping into small quenelle-shaped felafel.

Place the felafel on a baking sheet lined with parchment paper, drizzle with the remaining olive oil and bake for about 15 minutes.

Chickpea flatbread

Serves 4

Italian *farinata, cecina, torta de ceci* (depending on where you're from), or *socca* from just over the French border in Nice, is a flatbread made from chickpea flour. Trattorias and bakeries the length of the Riviera draw regular lunchtime queues, and back in my Italian yachting days I became a fan too.

200g/7oz/2 cups chickpea flour (gram flour/besan)

½ tbsp finely chopped rosemary (optional)

1 tsp salt

400ml/14fl oz/1⅔ cups water

3 tbsp extra-virgin olive oil

fried red onions and chunks of Gorgonzola, to serve

black pepper

Tip the chickpea flour, rosemary and salt into a large bowl and gradually whisk in the water until you have a loose, lump-free batter. Rest the batter for at least 1 hour and up to 12 (timing varies depending on the origin of the recipe, although I've noticed little difference in the results).

Preheat the oven to 220°C/425°F/gas mark 7.

Take a large flat pan or ovenproof frying pan (the professionals have a huge round pan specifically for the purpose) and heat it up in the oven or over a medium-high heat.

Skim off any froth from the top of the batter and then stir in most of the olive oil.

Add the remaining oil to the hot pan, swirling it to create a non-stick surface. Tip in the batter to a depth of about 1cm/½ inch and place in the oven. Bake for 15–20 minutes or until the surface is crisp and bubbling. I also give it a quick blast under the grill for some extra colour.

Top with fried red onions and Gorgonzola and give it a few turns of the pepper mill. Slice up with a pizza cutter and serve right away.

Cannellini, Parmesan and basil frittelle

**Makes 8 large or
16–20 canapé-size fritters**

olive oil for frying
1 onion, diced
2 garlic cloves, crushed
500g/1lb 2oz home-cooked
cannellini beans, or 2 x 400g/
14oz cans cannellini beans, rinsed
75g/2½oz Parmesan
cheese, grated
100g/3½oz mozzarella, very
finely chopped
zest of ½ lemon
juice of ½ lemon
2 tbsp fresh breadcrumbs
1 egg, lightly beaten
large handful of basil
leaves, ripped
salt and pepper
3-4 tbsp flour, for dusting
tomato salsa, to serve

Creamy white beans with plenty of cheese, seasoning and herbs make fabulous little fritters that virtually melt in your mouth. They're delicious with a fresh tomato salsa.

Heat 2 tablespoons of the olive oil in a large frying pan and cook the onion until soft and golden. Add the garlic and, as soon as you're engulfed in its wonderful smell, remove the pan from the heat and set aside.

Tip about two-thirds of the beans into a food processor, add the cooked onion and garlic and all the remaining fritter ingredients, except the flour and reserved beans. Pulse the mixture until it is fairly sticky but still has some texture. Remove the blade and stir in the whole beans. If mod cons aren't your thing, mash the beans with a fork or potato masher.

Now shape a small spoonful of the mixture into a small patty (it only need be the size of a large coin) and dust it with flour. Wipe the frying pan with a piece of paper towel and heat up a little oil. Cook the patty until deep gold, turning after a couple of minutes. Taste the cooked patty; you may need to balance the flavours of the bean mixture with more lemon, Parmesan, basil, salt or pepper. Rest the remaining mixture in the refrigerator for about 15 minutes to make it firmer and easier to handle.

Shape the mixture into equal-size patties and shallow-fry a few at a time; keep them somewhere warm until you have cooked the lot. Serve at once with a tomato salsa.

Tuscan cannellini with tomato and sage

Serves 6

By August, Italian markets are stacked with wooden crates of fresh borlotti and cannellini beans. Every region has its own particular way of cooking them, which, being Italy, is of course quite simply the only way.

500g/1lb 2oz/generous 2½ cups dried cannellini beans, soaked overnight (or, if you're very lucky, 500g/1lb 2oz fresh podded cannellini beans)

2 sprigs of sage

salt and pepper

5 tbsp extra-virgin olive oil

3 garlic cloves, halved

8 ripe tomatoes, peeled and chopped

grilled meats, sausages or bruschetta, to serve

Place the drained (or fresh) beans in a pan, and cover by 5cm/2 inch water. Throw in a sprig of sage, bring the water to the boil for 5 minutes, and then reduce to a simmer and cook until the beans are tender (anything between 30 minutes for fresh and 1½ hours for dried). Top up the water if the beans begin to emerge from the surface, but keep in mind that the beans should be juicy but not too soupy. Add some salt as the beans begin to soften.

Meanwhile, heat the oil very gently with the garlic and remaining sage. The idea is to infuse the garlic and sage flavours, but not lose the wonderful flavour of the extra-virgin olive oil. Stir in the tomatoes and simmer gently for a few minutes.

Add the tomatoes and sage to the beans, season with salt and pepper, cover and heat gently for about 15 minutes.

Serve with grilled meats, sausages or alone on a large slice of bruschetta.

Spiced vegetable fritters

Serves 4

Indian pakora, delicious deep-fried titbits in a light crisp batter, use a lightly spiced batter made with chickpea flour, or even pea or fava bean flour.

150g/5½oz/scant 1½ cups chickpea flour

½–1 tsp salt

½ tsp ground turmeric

1 tsp ground coriander

1 tsp garam masala

½ tsp chilli powder or cayenne pepper

about 150ml/5fl oz/²⁄₃ cup water

¼ tsp bicarbonate of soda

2 tbsp poppy seeds or 1 tsp nigella seeds (optional)

vegetable oil, for deep-frying

1 lemon or lime, cut into wedges

about 500g/1lb 2oz prepared vegetables, such as onion rings, cauliflower or broccoli florets, potato skins, sliced aubergine (eggplant), sweet potato or pumpkin chips, mushrooms

Put the chickpea flour, ½ tsp salt and the spices into a large bowl and gradually whisk in the water until you have a thick, smooth batter. Leave to stand for about 10 minutes.

Just before using the batter, stir in the bicarbonate of soda and poppy or nigella seeds, if using.

Pour the vegetable oil, to a depth of about 20cm/ 8 inches, into a large deep-fat fryer or heavy-bottomed wok. Heat the oil to 180°C/350°F. Test with a piece of vegetable dipped in the batter: it should sizzle and rise to the surface. Cook for about 8 minutes, then drain on kitchen paper, leave to cool slightly so you don't burn your mouth, and taste; you may want to add extra salt or spices to the batter.

Dip 3 or 4 pieces of vegetable into the batter and then drop them carefully into the hot oil; carry on dipping and adding until the surface of the oil is full but not crowded. Cook for about 8 minutes, carefully stirring every now and then, until the vegetables are crisp and golden. Using a slotted spoon, lift them out of the oil and drain on kitchen paper. Repeat until all the fritters are cooked.

Serve hot with lemon or lime wedges.

Black bean quesadillas

**Serves 4 as a main,
8 as a starter or snack**

The Tex-Mex answer to a stuffed crêpe, this is a wheat-flour tortilla stuffed with cheese and whatever else comes to hand. American recipes call for Monterey Jack cheese, or sometimes Cheddar, but Wensleydale works wonderfully. The black beans make these quesadillas more substantial – great for a brunch with all the guacamole, salsa and sour cream trimmings.

150g/5½oz Wensleydale cheese, or Cheddar at a pinch, crumbled

6 spring onions (scallions), sliced

500g/1lb 2oz home-cooked black beans, or 2 x 400g/14oz cans black beans, rinsed

4–5 pickled jalapeño peppers (from a jar), sliced (optional)

small handful of coriander (cilantro) leaves, finely chopped

salt and pepper

8 soft tortillas

To serve:
tomato salsa
guacamole
sour cream

Mix together the cheese, spring onions, beans, jalapeños and coriander leaves. Season to taste with salt and pepper.

Divide the mixture among the tortillas and fold them over to form a half moon shape. You can do this ahead of time.

Heat a ridged griddle or heavy frying pan, no oil required, and then cook the quesadillas two at a time until heated through.

Serve immediately or keep warm in the oven while you finish cooking the remaining quesadillas. Serve with a tomato salsa, guacamole and sour cream.

Celeriac and Puy lentil remoulade

Serves 4

The French answer to coleslaw, celeriac remoulade is a bistro classic. Here the lentils give extra texture and body, and, served with some good fresh bread, I'd be happy eating this for a light lunch.

200g/7oz/1 cup Puy lentils, rinsed
1 bay leaf
1 celeriac, about 700g/1lb 9 oz, peeled and trimmed
juice of ½ lemon
salt and pepper
2 tbsp roughly chopped fresh parsley
2 tbsp capers, roughly chopped

For the dressing:
5 tbsp mayonnaise, bought or home-made
1-2 tbsp Dijon mustard
2 tbsp crème fraîche

Put the lentils in a saucepan with the bay leaf and add cold water to cover by about 5cm/2 inches. Bring to the boil and then simmer for about 20 minutes, until tender but still intact. You may need to add a dash more water, so keep an eye on the lentils.

Meanwhile, cut the celeriac into matchsticks, throw it into a bowl and toss it around in the lemon juice.

Drain the lentils if necessary (I sometimes find that I have miraculously added the perfect amount of water), remove the bay leaf and season with a little salt and pepper.

To make the dressing, mix together the mayonnaise, mustard and crème fraîche, and season with salt and a good grind of black pepper. The dressing should be tart, creamy and thick enough to cling to the celeriac and lentils.

Stir the celeriac, lentils, parsley, capers and dressing together, taste and adjust the seasoning. Serve within a few hours of making: the celeriac becomes soft and pappy after a while.

Greek black-eyed peas with fennel and greens

Serves 6–8

Black-eyed peas and wild greens are a classic Greek combination. Black-eyed peas cook relatively quickly, especially when pre-boiled as here. Hence this is a cook-from-scratch rather than open-the-can recipe.

250g/9oz/1¼ cups dried black-eyed peas, rinsed

3 tbsp olive oil

2 onions, finely diced

2 carrots, diced

1 bulb of fennel, halved, cored and really finely sliced

4 garlic cloves, crushed

1 tsp fennel seeds, lightly bruised

2 tsp sweet Aleppo chilli flakes or ½ tsp hot chilli flakes

1 bay leaf

salt and pepper

300g/10½oz mixed greens such as Swiss chard, kale, spinach or beetroot (beet) leaves

3 tbsp tomato purée (tomato paste)

juice of 1 lemon

Place the beans in a saucepan, add enough water to cover by about 5cm/2 inches. Bring to the boil and boil for 5 minutes. Remove the pan from the heat.

Meanwhile, heat the oil in a large saucepan and add the onions, carrots and fennel. Stir over a medium heat until they begin to colour and then add the garlic, fennel seeds, chilli flakes and bay leaf. As soon as you can smell the garlic, turn down the heat, give the pan a good stir and cover with a tight-fitting lid. Cook very gently for about 15 minutes, taking care that the garlic does not catch or burn.

Drain the beans and then add them to the vegetables, adding enough water to cover by about 5cm/2 inches. Cover and simmer gently for anything between 30 minutes and 1 hour, checking from time to time whether you need to top up the water. The beans should be moist but not too soupy by the time they are tender. (You can drain away some of the broth if they seem too wet.) Add a large pinch of salt.

When the beans are just ready, add the greens and the tomato purée to the pan. Cook until the greens have wilted and then taste and adjust the seasoning with salt, pepper and lemon juice.

Quick supper beans

Serves 4–6

Super speedy and infinitely flexible, here's the way to magic up a bowl of tasty beans at a moment's notice. Equally happy alongside a fillet steak or an after-school fish finger.

2 tbsp olive oil
1 onion, roughly chopped
2 x 400g/14oz cans any cooked beans, rinsed, or about 500g/1lb 2oz home-cooked beans
2 garlic cloves, crushed (optional)
salt and pepper
2–3 tbsp extra-virgin olive oil

Heat the olive oil in a large pan and cook the onion until golden. Add half of the beans and really squash them around with the back of a wooden spoon, allowing them to catch and colour in places.

Stir in the remaining beans and the garlic, and cook until everything is heated through and smells fabulous. Season with salt and pepper to taste and add a couple of tablespoons of extra-virgin olive oil to add richness.

Now's the time to get creative, but remember that just a couple of additions will work better than ten.

How about?
... adding finely chopped parsley, basil, tarragon, rosemary, sage or thyme.
... throwing in some grated Parmesan, pecorino or lemon zest.
... tarting things up with capers, olives, anchovies or sunblush tomatoes.
... zipping it up with lemon juice, verjuice, balsamic or wine vinegar.
... spicing it up with roasted cumin seeds, smoked paprika, sweet chilli flakes or ras el hanout.

Stir-fried greens with fermented black beans

Serves 4 as a side dish

These greens are spectacularly good and have such a depth of savoury umami flavour that I could happily dive into a pile with some boiled white rice and call it a day. However, the combination of this stir-fry with roast belly pork, Chinese-style pork spare ribs or the more authentic *cha siu* (sticky sweet roast pork), if you happen to live near Chinatown, is out of this world. You could stir in some marinated and fried tofu or tempeh for a delicious vegan alternative.

250g/9oz mixture of pak choi (bok choy), spring greens and purple sprouting broccoli

2 tbsp vegetable oil

2 garlic cloves, sliced

1 tbsp grated fresh ginger

1–2 fresh red chillies, finely sliced, seeds in or out

1 tbsp fermented black beans, rinsed and drained

1–2 tsp light soy sauce

1 tsp sugar (optional)

Quarter the pak choi, slice the spring greens or trim and divide the purple sprouting broccoli. Bring a pan of water to the boil and cook the vegetables for a couple of minutes, until just tender. Refresh in cold water and then drain.

Heat the oil in a wok or large frying pan. Stir-fry the garlic, ginger and chilli until you're enveloped in wonderful smells – a matter of seconds, as you must not burn the garlic.

Throw in the black beans and greens and stir-fry over a high heat for a couple of minutes, adding a tablespoon of water if the pan gets dry. Taste and season with soy sauce and sugar if needed. Serve at once.

Soups & Salads

Pumpkin, coconut and lentil soup

Serves 4

2 tbsp vegetable oil

small bunch of spring onions (scallions), finely sliced

2 garlic cloves, crushed

5cm/2 inch piece of fresh ginger, chopped

1–2 fiery chillies, finely chopped

2 stalks of lemongrass, outer leaves removed and remainder finely sliced

225g/8oz/generous 1 cup red lentils, rinsed

500g/1lb 2oz pumpkin or butternut squash, peeled, deseeded and cut into 2cm/¾ inch dice

1.2 litres/2 pints/5 cups vegetable or chicken stock

400g/14oz can coconut milk

1 tbsp tamarind paste

2 tbsp finely chopped fresh coriander (cilantro)

Thai fish sauce or tamari soy sauce

juice of 1–2 limes

pinch of brown sugar or palm sugar (optional)

Pumpkin gives this soup a wonderful velvety texture and when it comes to the flavour, the Thai balance of spicy, sweet, sour and salty is vital. The chilli provides the spicy heat, so just keep adding small amounts of fish sauce or soy, lime juice and sugar until you reach perfection.

Heat the oil in a large saucepan and add most of the spring onions (setting aside a tablespoon to garnish). Add the garlic, ginger, chillies and lemongrass and stir for a minute or two, until you are engulfed in fabulous smells. You will be wheezing if you have been generous with the chilli!

Add the lentils, pumpkin or squash and the stock, and simmer until the lentils are soft and the pumpkin flesh has collapsed.

Stir in the coconut milk, tamarind and most of the coriander. Now taste and balance the soup with fish sauce or tamari, lime juice and sugar.

Serve hot, sprinkled with the remaining spring onions and coriander.

Chickpea, chilli and mint soup

Serves 4

Fast, easy, cheap and, above all, wonderfully, zippily delicious. This is a soup I always teach to teenagers on their student survival course. You can blitz it with a hand-held blender in the pan – so that's another plus – and there's barely any washing up, but if you have the time, this becomes beautifully silky and creamy if well whizzed in a jug blender.

3 tbsp olive oil

2 onions, diced

4 garlic cloves, finely chopped

2-3 red chillies, finely chopped

2 x 400g/14oz cans chickpeas (garbanzo beans), rinsed, or 500g/1lb 2oz home-cooked chickpeas

1 litre/1¾ pints/4 cups vegetable or chicken stock (a stock cube will do)

salt

juice of ½ –1 lemon

about 12 fresh mint leaves, sliced

Heat the oil in a large saucepan and cook the onions until golden. Add the garlic and chillies and, as soon as you can really smell the sizzling garlic, add the chickpeas and the stock and simmer for about 10 minutes.

Blitz the soup, using a hand-held blender for convenience or a jug blender for a smoother result.

Taste the soup; it will seem rather bland but adding salt, plenty of lemon juice and the mint will work wonders. Serve hot.

Tomato, rosemary and red lentil soup

Serves 4

A favourite standby recipe, I can usually rustle this up without a trip to the shops. It came about in a boatyard in Provence, where I had to feed hungry deckhands a hearty lunch. Crisp blue winter sky and fresh baguette apart, it still tastes pretty wonderful.

2 tbsp olive oil

1 onion, finely diced

2 garlic cloves, crushed

1 sprig of rosemary, leaves finely chopped

1–2 fresh chillies, very finely chopped, or a good pinch of dried chilli flakes

225g/8oz/generous 1 cup red lentils, rinsed

400g/14oz can chopped tomatoes

1.2 litres/2 pints/5 cups vegetable or chicken stock

salt

juice of 1–2 lemons

4 tbsp crème fraîche, sour cream or plant-based oat or soya cream

Heat the oil in a large saucepan and cook the onion gently until soft and translucent. Add the garlic, rosemary and just enough chilli to give the soup a nice little kick. Once you can smell the garlic and rosemary, add the lentils, tomatoes and stock and simmer for about 30 minutes, or until the lentils are soft.

If you feel that the soup is too thick, add a little water or stock. Taste and balance with salt and enough lemon juice to lift the soup: it should be really fresh and zippy. Serve hot, topped with a spoonful of crème fraîche or cream.

Squash, black bean and sweetcorn soup

Serves 4

A hearty, satisfying soup with vibrant fresh flavours. Serve it with sour cream, guacamole, corn tacos or toasted tortillas and you have a meal in a bowl.

2 tbsp olive oil

1 onion, diced

450g/1lb butternut squash, peeled, deseeded and cut into 5cm/2 inch chunks

2 garlic cloves, crushed

salt and pepper

1 tsp ground cumin

1 tsp sweet Spanish smoked paprika

½ tsp chilli flakes

400g/14oz can chopped tomatoes

300ml/10½fl oz/1¼ cups vegetable stock (a good cube or bouillon powder will do)

250g/9oz home-cooked black beans, or 400g/14oz can black beans, rinsed

200g/7oz sweetcorn kernels

Tabasco sauce (optional)

juice of ½–1 lime, or 1 tbsp wine vinegar (optional)

handful of fresh coriander (cilantro), chopped

150ml/5fl oz/⅔ cup sour cream

Heat the oil in a large saucepan and cook the onion until soft and beginning to colour. Add the squash and stir around for a couple of minutes. Toss in the garlic, a pinch of salt and the spices, and stir for about a minute, then tip in the tomatoes and stock. Simmer for about 15 minutes or until the squash is just tender.

Scoop out about half of the squash with a little of the liquid, place in a deep container and purée with a hand-held blender. You could use a potato masher or blitz all the soup in the saucepan, but I like the contrast of the large intact chunks of squash with the velvety soup. Return the puréed squash to the soup. Add the beans and sweetcorn, and a little water if the soup is very thick, and simmer for 5 minutes.

Taste and balance the flavours with salt, pepper or Tabasco, lime juice or wine vinegar. Serve in bowls, with a scattering of coriander and a large spoonful of sour cream.

Summer minestrone with pesto

Serves 6–8

This is a legume showcase with borlotti, broad beans, green beans and peas. Do vary the vegetables – that's the idea. Finely sliced fennel or Swiss chard would be delicious instead of, or as well as, any of the other greens.

2 tbsp olive oil
1 onion, diced
2 carrots, diced
2 celery stalks, diced
handful of green beans, sliced into 2cm/¾ inch pieces
handful of broad beans (fava beans), preferably skinned
handful of fresh or frozen peas
small bunch of asparagus, trimmed and sliced into 2cm/¾ inch pieces
1 courgette (zucchini), finely diced
salt and pepper
2 litres/3½ pints/2 quarts vegetable stock, or chicken stock for a richer result
250g/9oz home-cooked borlotti beans (cranberry beans), or 400g/14oz can borlotti beans, rinsed
2 potatoes, cut into 2cm/¾ inch dice
100g/3½oz tiny pasta shapes such as ditalini or stelle
2 tomatoes, peeled, deseeded and diced
pesto, to serve

Heat the oil in a large saucepan and cook the onion, carrots and celery for about 5 minutes, until soft. Now add half of each of your green and broad beans, peas, asparagus and courgette, sprinkle with a little salt and stir around in the oil for a couple of minutes.

Add the stock and simmer for about 30 minutes. Don't worry about the texture of the vegetables, the idea is to flavour the soup.

Throw in the borlotti beans, potatoes and pasta, and simmer until the potato is beginning to soften.

Now add the remaining green vegetables and cook for about 5 minutes – you want these to remain fresh and al dente.

Taste and season with salt and pepper, then stir in the tomatoes. Serve the soup in bowls, with a large teaspoon of pesto in each.

Miso with soba noodles

Serves 4

Adding soba noodles turns this miso soup into a satisfying meal.

1 x 10cm/4 inch piece of dried kombu

1 litre/1¾ pints/4 cups water

4 x dried shitake mushrooms, covered in warm water and soaked for 15 minutes

1 carrot, sliced into matchsticks

150g/5½oz dried soba noodles

2–3 tbsp miso paste

300g/10½oz pak choi (bok choy), sliced

4 spring onions (scallions), finely sliced

1 tbsp toasted sesame seeds

Bring the kombu and water to the boil in a large saucepan. Pick out the mushrooms from their soaking liquid. If the liquid is gritty, strain it, then add it to the saucepan. Remove the stalks and slice the mushrooms. Add the mushrooms and the carrot to the pan and simmer for about 10 minutes.

Cook the noodles in lightly salted boiling water until tender (4–5 minutes). Drain and rinse in cool water.

Discard the kombu from the stock pan. Put the miso paste in a small bowl, ladle over some hot stock and stir until the miso has dissolved. Add the pak choi to the stock pan and bring to the boil. As soon as the leaves have softened, turn down the heat and add the noodles and the miso.

Serve in bowls, topped with the spring onions and sesame seeds.

Chickpea, beetroot and feta salad

Serves 4

Chickpeas make this refreshing eastern Mediterranean salad substantial enough to eat as a main course along with toasted pitta.

½ red onion, sliced

2 tbsp red wine vinegar

4 tbsp extra-virgin olive oil, plus extra to serve

3 garlic cloves, halved

500g/1lb 2oz home-cooked chickpeas (garbanzo beans), or 2 x 400g/14oz cans chickpeas, rinsed

salt and pepper

1 tbsp sesame seeds

1 tsp fennel seeds

200g/7oz feta cheese, cut into 2.5cm/1 inch dice

100g/3½oz baby spinach or other salad leaves

½ cucumber, diced

large bunch of flat-leaf parsley, chopped

about 20 fresh mint leaves

2 small cooked beetroot (beets), roughly diced

seeds from 1 pomegranate

toasted pitta or sourdough, to serve

Soak the onion in the vinegar; it will turn a glorious fuchsia pink and become softer and more digestible.

Gently warm the olive oil and garlic in a saucepan for 5 minutes. The idea is not to fry the garlic but to infuse the oil and soften the garlic's flavour. Remove the pan from the heat, take out the garlic, chop it finely and return it to the pan along with the chickpeas. Stir them in the warm oil, season with a little salt and pepper, and then set aside to cool.

In a dry frying pan, toast the sesame and fennel seeds until the sesame seeds dance around and turn gold. Tip the seeds onto a plate and carefully toss the feta around to coat each dice in a speckled crust.

Put the onion with the vinegar and the chickpeas with their garlic oil with the salad leaves, cucumber, parsley and most of the mint in a serving bowl and mix carefully. Now add the feta and beetroot and toss gently just a couple of times, otherwise the entire salad will turn a milky pink. Taste and adjust the seasoning if necessary.

Sprinkle with pomegranate seeds and a few mint leaves and serve with toasted pitta or sourdough bread and a dash of extra-virgin olive oil.

Hot-smoked salmon, egg and lentil salad

Serves 4

A wonderful light summer lunch. Everything can be prepared ahead and then assembled just before serving.

200g/7oz fine green beans, topped but not tailed

4 cornichons or small gherkins, sliced

4 x 85g/3oz fillets of hot-smoked salmon, flaked into large pieces

3 eggs, boiled for 6 minutes, shelled and quartered

For the lentils:

250g/9oz/1¼ cups Puy lentils, or Castelluccio, rinsed

1 bay leaf

6 spring onions (scallions), finely sliced

2 tbsp red wine vinegar

1 garlic clove, crushed

4 tbsp extra-virgin olive oil

4 tbsp flat-leaf parsley

salt and pepper

For the herby crème fraîche:

3 tbsp crème fraîche

1 tbsp finely chopped fresh dill

1 tbsp finely chopped fresh parsley

2 tsp grainy mustard

First prepare the lentils. Put the lentils in a pan with the bay leaf and cover with water. Bring to the boil and then simmer for about 20–30 minutes, until tender but still intact. Drain, reserving the cooking liquid, and while still warm add the spring onions, vinegar, garlic and olive oil. Season with salt and pepper. Leave to cool then stir in the parsley and if it seems dry, add a little of the cooking water. Transfer to a serving bowl.

Meanwhile, steam or boil the green beans until just tender and then refresh them under cold water to keep them crisp and bright. Drain well. Stir the green beans and cornichons through the lentil salad, taste and check the seasoning.

Mix together the crème fraîche, herbs and mustard and season to taste. Crème fraîche is naturally slightly sour, but you might want to add a dash of vinegar or lemon juice.

Arrange the salmon and eggs on top of the lentils and serve with a spoonful of the herby crème fraîche.

Spiced lentil salad

Serves 6–8

I came across *My New Roots,* Sarah Britton's fabulous food blog, while surfing the internet for lentil inspiration. I could hardly bypass a recipe with the title 'The Best Lentil Salad, Ever'. It lived up to expectations and has had many reincarnations since.

500g/1lb 2oz/generous 2½ cups Puy lentils, rinsed

1 red onion, finely diced

150g/5½oz/scant 1 cup currants, sultanas (golden raisins) or other dried fruit, diced to lentil size

4 heaped tbsp capers, rinsed (and diced if large)

For the vinaigrette:

6 tbsp extra-virgin olive oil

4 tbsp apple cider vinegar

1 tbsp maple syrup

1 tbsp Dijon mustard

2 tsp each of salt and pepper

1 tsp ground cumin

½ tsp ground turmeric

½ tsp ground coriander

½ tsp ground cardamom

¼ tsp cayenne pepper

¼ tsp ground cloves

¼ tsp freshly grated nutmeg

¼ tsp ground cinnamon

Put the lentils in a saucepan and cover with about 5cm/2 inch cold water. Bring to the boil and then simmer until tender, but still with a bit of bite; this can take anything from 15–25 minutes.

Meanwhile, place all the vinaigrette ingredients in a jar and give it a good shake.

Once cooked, drain the lentils and rinse briefly with a little cold water to stop them overcooking and turning soggy.

While still just warm, combine the lentils with the onion, dried fruit, capers and vinaigrette. Eat right away or, alternatively, the salad will keep for a couple of days in the refrigerator – it tastes all the better for a bit of resting.

You can also add fresh leaves, vegetables, cheese or whatever else takes your fancy at the last minute.

Smoked mackerel, grapefruit and lentil salad

Serves 4

The mackerel/grapefruit pairing leapt out of a magazine when I was at the hairdresser's. The super-healthy salad article promised me a waspish waistline in a matter of weeks along with increased powers of concentration. I'm still waiting. Health issues aside, the combination is divine, especially with a bit of avocado thrown in.

2 grapefruits, preferably pink

2 ripe avocados, skins removed and pitted

small bunch of watercress, washed and stalks removed

½ x Spiced Lentil Salad (see page 90)

4 fillets of smoked mackerel, skin removed

2 tbsp toasted pumpkin seeds

black pepper, to taste

Using a small serrated knife, slice off the top and bottom of the grapefruit and then cut away all the skin and pith. Holding the grapefruit over a bowl to catch the juice, saw the knife carefully back and forth along the membrane that separates the segments until you reach the centre, turn the knife so you have effectively cut a V shape and out will drop the segment. Continue until you have removed all the flesh. Set the segments aside separately from the juice.

Slice the avocados and stir gently in the bowl of grapefruit juice so that it doesn't oxidize and brown.

Add about half of the grapefruit, avocado and watercress to the lentil salad and flake in some of the mackerel. Fold rather than stir the salad very gently so that everything stays intact.

Place the salad in a wide bowl, or on individual plates, and scatter with the reserved ingredients, including the grapefruit juice and the pumpkin seeds. Taste; it's unlikely that you'll need any more salt as the fish will be salty, but plenty of black pepper will really lift the flavour.

Sprouting bean and quinoa salad

Serves 4

Oh, I know, all this superfood business is a bit of a cliché, but honestly you will have good reason to feel healthy and rather self-righteous after eating this salad. Most of these ingredients are vying for pole position in the world superfood ratings.

200g/7oz/generous 1 cup quinoa, well rinsed

4 tbsp extra-virgin olive oil

2 tbsp red wine vinegar

salt and pepper

200g/7oz sprouting beans,

½ red onion, diced

3–4 large sprigs of dill, stalks removed, roughly chopped

10 mint leaves, ripped up roughly

100g/3½oz baby spinach

1 pomegranate, seeds and juice but no pithy membrane

3 oranges, cut into segments

200g/7oz feta cheese or cashew nut 'cheese', crumbled

Boil the quinoa in about 300ml/10½fl oz/1¼ cups of water for about 15 minutes, until the grain has swelled up and you can see a Saturn-like ring around it. Drain off any excess moisture. While still warm, add the oil, vinegar and salt and pepper to taste. Set aside to cool.

Now toss the sprouting beans together with the onion, dill, mint, spinach, pomegranate and orange. Spoon out about a quarter of the mixture to use as a garnish, and then carefully tumble in the quinoa and half of the feta. Taste and balance the flavours with salt, pepper, vinegar and extra-virgin olive oil.

Serve, topped with the remaining feta and the reserved technicolor bean mixture.

Bean and tomato salad with ginger, chilli and herbs

Serves 4

This salad comes from the Bertinet Kitchen in Bath, where I teach. We serve it alongside cured meats, cheese, pots of goodies such as tapenade and chickpea purée (and some fabulous bread of course – we're talking French baker extraordinaire); the perfect lunch. The antithesis of the 1970s stodgy bean salad, this is fresh, zippy and packed with vitamins. There's another bonus too: it takes about 5 minutes to prepare.

2 shallots, finely sliced

4cm/1½ inch piece of fresh ginger, finely diced

1–2 red or green chillies, very finely diced

4 tomatoes, quartered

handful of fresh basil, coriander (cilantro) or any other herb, roughly chopped

2 x 400g/14oz cans mixed beans, rinsed, or 500g/1lb 2oz home-cooked beans

juice of ½ lemon or lime

1 tbsp red wine vinegar

extra-virgin olive oil

salt and pepper

Place all the ingredients in a large bowl, toss everything together, taste and balance the salt, pepper, acidity and oil.

Zippy Indian chickpea and potato salad

Serves 6–8

350g/12oz potatoes, cut into large pieces

250g/9oz home-cooked chickpeas (garbanzo beans), or 400g/14oz can chickpeas, rinsed

4 tomatoes, diced

10cm/4 inch piece of cucumber, diced

2.5cm/1 inch piece of fresh ginger, finely diced

½–1 red onion, finely diced

3–4 fresh green chillies, finely diced

juice of 2 limes

1 tsp salt

1 tsp brown sugar or jaggery

1 tsp cumin seeds

1 tsp coriander seeds

1 tsp amchur (sour green mango powder), or perhaps a dash more lime juice

large handful of fresh coriander (cilantro), roughly chopped

All or any of the following (optional):

2 carrots, grated

1 small mango, diced (a 'green' or unripe mango would be fabulous)

100g/3½oz raw beetroot (beet), grated

Fast food, the Indian way. All over India, small carts line the roadside selling delicious savoury snacks, or *chaat*, such as this hot and sour salad. The ingredients are usually mixed to order, keeping every customer happy. You can do the same at home, holding back on the chilli, lime juice and spices for the less adventurous.

Boil the potatoes in salted water until just tender and then dice roughly.

Meanwhile, put the chickpeas in a large serving bowl with the tomatoes, cucumber, ginger and onion.

Traditionally this is a dish with a good kick, but taste the tip of one of the chillies and decide how much you want to add. Stir in the lime juice, salt, sugar and spices.

Stir in the potatoes, any fruit or vegetable options, and the coriander. Taste and adjust the seasoning: this should be mouth-puckeringly sour.

You can serve the salad with yogurt (coconut yogurt is delicious) and flatbread, ideally roti, but toasted pitta will do fine.

Asian-style three-bean salad

Serves 4

Soya, mung and adzuki are the three great beans of the East. Soya has been consumed for thousands of years as tofu and in its fermented incarnations such as soy sauce and tempeh. Mung beans are most commonly eaten as bean sprouts, adding their crisp texture to salads and stir-fries, but here we enjoy them cooked.

100g/3½oz dried adzuki beans or 200g/7oz cooked beans

100g/3½oz dried mung beans or 200g/7oz cooked beans

250g/9oz edamame (fresh or frozen)

2 spring onions (scallions), finely sliced

2 red (bell) peppers, finely diced

1 daikon (mooli/Japanese radish), peeled and finely diced (optional)

For the dressing:

2 tbsp white miso paste

2 tbsp grated fresh ginger

2 tbsp Japanese soy sauce

2 tbsp mirin (or white wine vinegar and 1 tsp sugar)

4 tbsp rapeseed or other vegetable oil

1–2 tbsp sesame oil

salt and pepper

Rinse the dried beans, if using, and in separate pans, cover them with plenty of cold water and bring to the boil. Skim off any foamy scum and then turn down to a simmer. The beans will take anything from 20 minutes to 1 hour, depending on their age. They should be tender but still holding together well, or your salad will be a sludge. Drain the beans and set aside to cool. Alternatively, use ready-cooked beans.

Plunge the edamame into salted boiling water, or steam them for about 3 minutes. Drain and rinse with cold water to stop them cooking further.

Mix together all the dressing ingredients with a good pinch of salt and plenty of black pepper. Taste – you may need more salt, pepper, vinegar or even a pinch of sugar.

Place all the beans in a serving bowl with the spring onions, red peppers and daikon, if using (do try it, the texture is fabulous). Pour over the dressing and tumble everything together, taking care not to mash up the beans. If possible, leave for about 20 minutes for the flavours to marry and soak into the beans before serving.

Big Dishes

Roasted roots with chickpeas

Serves 4

Pomegranate molasses makes a fabulous Middle Eastern dressing with a touch of lemon juice and plenty of olive oil. Naturally sweet root vegetables and chickpeas make a great combination with the yogurt, but it's the pomegranate molasses and spices that lift this dish onto another plain.

400g/14oz carrots, preferably small ones, halved if large

3 parsnips, quartered lengthways, woody core removed

4 tbsp olive oil

salt and pepper

300g/10½oz beetroot (beet), peeled and cut into quarters or bite-size chunks

250g/9oz home-cooked chickpeas (garbanzo beans), or 400g/14oz can chickpeas, rinsed

4 tbsp pomegranate molasses

1 tsp caraway seeds

1 tsp cumin seeds

½ tsp chilli flakes or milder Aleppo chilli flakes

juice of 1 lemon

extra-virgin olive oil

large handful of flat-leaf parsley or coriander (cilantro), or a mixture of both, chopped

250g/9oz Greek-style yogurt

Preheat the oven to 200°C/400°F/gas mark 6. Toss the carrots and parsnips in a large roasting pan with 2 tablespoons of the olive oil and a little salt. If the pan is large enough, use a small corner for the beetroot and toss that in the remaining oil; otherwise you will require a separate pan. Try not to toss the beetroot with the other vegetables at any stage, otherwise your entire dish will turn a rather unappetizing, lurid pink.

Roast the vegetables for about 15 minutes, then add the chickpeas. Turn the vegetables carefully and roll the chickpeas around to pick up any oil in the pan.

Roast for a further 10 minutes, then spoon over the molasses and scatter with the spices. Turn the vegetables in the sticky syrup and roast for a further 5–10 minutes, until just tender, but not soft, and starting to brown. Season well with salt, a bit more chilli or pepper, some lemon juice and a dash of extra-virgin olive oil.

Pile the vegetables on a large platter and scatter with the herbs. Serve hot or warm, with a bowl of yogurt to spoon out at the table.

Greek baked butter beans with feta

Serves 6

Try seeking out the signature supersize Greek *gigantes* beans for this if you have a local Greek grocer's or an especially well-stocked deli, or try online.

3 tbsp olive oil

1 large onion, roughly diced

2 carrots, diced

2 large celery stalks, diced

3 garlic cloves, crushed

400g/14oz can chopped tomatoes

2 tbsp tomato purée (tomato paste)

3 bay leaves

½ tsp dried chilli flakes

salt

½ tsp dried oregano

large bunch of parsley, roughly chopped

3 sprigs of dill, stems removed, roughly chopped

½ tbsp brown sugar or honey

1 tbsp red wine vinegar

1kg/2¼lb home-cooked gigantes or large butter beans (large lima beans), or 4 x 400g/14oz cans butter beans, rinsed

200g/7oz feta cheese, crumbled

Preheat the oven to 180°C/350°F/gas mark 4. Heat the oil in a large pan and cook the onion, carrots and celery gently until they soften and begin to colour. Add the garlic, stir until fragrant, then tip in the tomatoes, tomato purée, bay leaves and chilli flakes. Season with a good pinch of salt, add the oregano and most of the parsley and dill, and leave to bubble away for about 10 minutes.

Taste, keeping in mind that you will be adding a large quantity of beans that require plenty of acidity and savoury seasoning. Balance the sauce, adding the sugar and vinegar, or to taste.

Add the beans. Now all the soakers and simmerers among you can feel rather smug as you can add enough of the nutrient-rich bean cooking water to just cover the beans. Otherwise use tap water. Tip the beans into a wide, ovenproof dish and place in the oven for about 1 hour.

After 30 minutes, check that the beans still have plenty of liquid; the juices will have thickened, but you don't want the beans to dry out. The top needs to become a bit crispy and crunchy while the beans wallow in delicious juices. Sprinkle the feta over with the remaining herbs and serve hot or warm.

Middle Eastern fava beans

Serves 4

Ful medames is not just the national dish of Egypt, it's hugely popular from Sudan right up through the Middle East to Syria. The beans are often eaten at breakfast time, particularly during the Ramadan fast, when a plate of fuls can just about keep you going until nightfall.

500g/1lb 2oz home-cooked whole fava beans, or 3 x 400g/14oz cans ful beans (cooked fava beans), rinsed

salt and pepper

2 garlic cloves, crushed

150ml/5fl oz/⅔ cup extra-virgin olive oil

juice of 1–2 lemons

1–2 tsp cumin seeds, roasted and ground

pitta bread, to serve

Garnishes – any of the following:

fresh tomatoes, diced

sliced spring onions (scallions) or, more traditionally, wedges of white onion

handful of rocket (arugula)

fresh coriander (cilantro) or parsley, roughly chopped

hard-boiled eggs

black olives

Aleppo or Urfa chilli flakes

tahini

extra-virgin olive oil

Heat the beans with plenty of seasoning. If using cans, just tip their liquid into the saucepan with them. If you've cooked your own beans, make sure that they are really tender and almost mushy.

Drain off some of the cooking liquid, leaving behind just a few tablespoons with the beans. Stir in the garlic, olive oil, lemon juice and cumin to taste. Spoon into bowls and serve.

This simple combination makes a wonderfully sustaining dish scooped up with flatbread, but you can turn it into a feast with a selection of the garnishes set out in small bowls so that everyone can help themselves. Everyone loves to get stuck in, making up their own magical combination.

Indian stir-fried sprouted beans

Serves 4

Sprouting beans for cooking has been a revelation to me (see pages 20–21). Yes, you do have to be quite organized, but the nutty texture and taste of these beans is just fabulous. Moth beans are extraordinary: soak overnight and sprout for one day and these little powerhouses are ready to go. If you have trouble finding moth (matki) beans, then use sprouted mung beans or adzuki instead.

200g/7oz dried moth beans, soaked and sprouted (or sprouted adzuki or mung beans)

2–3 tbsp vegetable oil

handful of raw peanuts

1 tsp cumin seeds

1 tsp black mustard seeds

10 curry leaves

1 onion, diced

2.5cm/1 inch piece of fresh ginger, finely chopped

2 garlic cloves, crushed

1 tsp garam masala,

½ tsp chilli powder

1–2 tsp light brown sugar or jaggery

1 tsp salt

handful of fresh coriander (cilantro), chopped

1 lime, quartered

rice or chapatis, to serve

Rinse the sprouted beans and put them in a pan, cover them with plenty of cold water and boil for about 10 minutes until tender. Drain.

Meanwhile, heat the oil in a karahi, wok or frying pan, and fry the peanuts for a couple of minutes, until golden. Scoop out the nuts and set aside.

In the same oil, heat the cumin and mustard seeds until they begin to hop about. Add the curry leaves and onion and cook until the onion is soft and turning golden.

Now add the ginger, garlic, garam masala, chilli powder, sugar and salt. As soon as you smell the amazing spicy aromas, you can throw in the drained beans. Stir to coat in the spices and then add a slosh of water to prevent them from catching on the bottom of the pan. The amount of liquid is up to you. You could serve it quite wet, with a bit of soupy sauce to mop up, or you may prefer to leave it a little drier, as I do. Cook over a high heat for a couple of minutes, taste and then season with sugar and salt.

Sprinkle with the roasted peanuts and coriander and serve with wedges of lime and rice or chapatis.

Keralan aubergines with lentils, cashew and tamarind

Serves 4

Small, egg-shaped aubergines are often available in Indian grocer's and are worth seeking out for this dish. They look beautiful, opened out like paper lanterns.

3 large or 8–12 baby, egg-shaped aubergines (eggplants)

1 tbsp vegetable oil, plus extra for brushing

2 onions, finely diced

5 garlic cloves, crushed

5cm/2 inch piece of fresh ginger, diced

2 tsp dried chilli flakes

100g/3½oz/½ cup red split lentils (masoor dal), rinsed

½ tsp cumin seeds, roasted and ground

salt

3 tbsp dairy or coconut yogurt

3–4 tbsp tamarind paste

handful of coriander (cilantro) leaves

3 tbsp cashew nuts, roasted

flatbreads or rice, to serve

On the top (optional):

2 tbsp ghee or vegetable oil

1 tbsp mustard seeds

4 dried chillies

Preheat the oven to 200°C/400°F/gas mark 6. Prick the aubergines once or twice, brush with a little oil, and roast in the oven until they are soft (about 30 minutes for regular aubergines, 15 minutes for the egg-size ones). Cool for a few minutes.

Meanwhile, heat the vegetable oil in a large frying pan and cook the onions gently until translucent. Add the garlic, ginger and chilli flakes and, once you are enveloped by the wafts of garlic, tip in the lentils and enough water to cover by 5cm/2 inches. Simmer the lentils for about 20 minutes, until they are soft and creamy. Stir in the cumin and season with salt.

Cut the large aubergines lengthways into quarters. For the egg-shaped aubergines, hold them by their stalks and make vertical slashes, leaving the base and top intact. Push down on the stalk, and the skin will open up like a Chinese lantern. Add the aubergines to the lentils, pushing them down halfway.

Dollop over the yogurt and tamarind. Don't stir them in, the idea is to get bursts of different flavours. Sprinkle with coriander and cashews. Just before serving, melt the ghee, and heat the mustard seeds and dried chillies until they sizzle and pop. Tip over the aubergines and eat with Indian flatbreads or rice.

Flageolets with kale and crisped potatoes

Serves 4

I can't get enough of San Francisco-based Heidi Swanson's recipes; her blog *101 Cookbooks* is truly inspiring. While Heidi is a vegetarian crusader for natural wholefoods, her food never seems remotely 'worthy'. This dish evolved out of the White Beans and Cabbage recipe from her book *Super Natural Every Day*.

3 tbsp olive oil

1 large potato, cut into 2cm/¾ inch dice

salt and pepper

1 small red onion, finely sliced

250g/9oz home-cooked flageolets or 400g/14oz can flageolet beans, rinsed

2 garlic cloves, finely chopped

200g/7oz kale, tough stalks removed, sliced into ribbons

juice of ½–1 lemon

5 tbsp grated Parmesan cheese

Heat the olive oil in a large frying pan (with a lid) over a medium-high heat. Toss in the potato and a pinch of salt. Cover the pan and cook for a few minutes, then carefully turn the potatoes. Continue until the potatoes are golden, crisp and cooked through.

Add the onion and beans to the pan, and carry on cooking, with the lid off. Leave the beans to brown and catch a little on the bottom of the pan. You will want to stir – don't!

After a couple of minutes, when the onion has softened and the beans have a few golden, crusty flecks, stir in the garlic and the kale. Reduce the heat slightly and cover the pan.

The kale will take about 3 minutes to wilt, and then you are ready to taste and season. Add salt and plenty of coarsely ground black pepper, lemon juice and a good sprinkling of Parmesan, and serve.

Tarka dal

Serves 8 as a side dish, 4 as a main with flatbread or rice

400g/14oz/2 cups moong dal, masoor dal, or a mixture of both

1.2 litres/2 pints/5 cups water

5cm/2 inch piece of fresh ginger, chopped

3 garlic cloves, finely chopped

1 tsp ground turmeric

½-1 tsp salt

squeeze of lemon juice (optional)

2 tbsp roughly chopped fresh coriander (cilantro)

For the tarka:

2 generous tbsp ghee, butter or vegetable oil

1 red onion, sliced

3-4 fresh green chillies, sliced

Wash the dal thoroughly and check for any tiny stones. Place them in a large saucepan with the water. Bring them to the boil and skim away any frothy scum.

Throw in the ginger, garlic and turmeric and simmer, with the lid ajar, on the lowest heat possible for about 1½ hours. (A ridged griddle pan can help to diffuse the heat if you have a particularly fierce gas hob, just put your saucepan on top.) Stir from time to time and add more water if the dal is very thick.

When the lentils have collapsed, taste and season with salt. Add more water if you like a soupy consistency; I prefer mine to be like a loose porridge.

For the tarka, heat the ghee, butter or oil in a small pan. (I would go for the luscious creaminess of ghee or butter every time.) Add the onion and cook until golden. Add the chillies and stir for a moment or two over a high heat. Tip the tarka over the dal, stir it in along with a squeeze of lemon juice, if using, and then sprinkle with coriander.

Tarkas to try – add to the ghee, butter or oil:
- 3 diced shallots or ½ onion, 2 tsp cumin seeds, 1 tsp black mustard seeds
- 1 tbsp grated fresh ginger, 2 finely sliced garlic cloves, diced flesh of 3 tomatoes
- 1 tsp black mustard seeds, about 8 curry leaves, ½-1 tsp crushed chilli flakes
- 3 garlic cloves, finely sliced

Orange pan-glazed tempeh

Serves 4

This recipe is well travelled. It comes from the thoroughly inspiring Australian chef and food writer Jude Blereau's book *Coming Home to Eat: Wholefood for the Family*. If you're a tempeh virgin, then let this be your first tantalizingly tasty experience. I love to serve this simply, with steamed greens and a few fine slices of red chilli thrown in. If you're feeling hungry, cook up a bit of rice, too.

1 tbsp grated fresh ginger

250ml/9fl oz/1 cup fresh orange juice

2 tsp tamari soy sauce

1½ tbsp mirin

2 tsp maple syrup

½ tsp ground coriander

2 garlic cloves, crushed

300g/10½oz tempeh

2 tbsp extra-virgin olive oil or, better still, unrefined coconut oil

large handful of coriander (cilantro) leaves

juice of ½ lime

Squeeze the juice from the grated ginger into a bowl. I find it easiest to pile up the ginger in the middle of a small square of muslin (cheesecloth), gather up the edges and then twist the cloth into a tight ball until the juice runs out. Discard the pulp.

Add the orange juice to the bowl along with the tamari, mirin, maple syrup, ground coriander and garlic. Stir everything together and then set aside.

Chop up the tempeh into thin-ish, bite-size slithers, triangles, fingers or whatever shape takes your fancy.

Heat the oil in a large frying pan until hot, but not smoking, and cook the tempeh for about 5 minutes on each side until golden.

Pour the orange juice mixture into the pan and simmer for 10 minutes, until the sauce has reduced to a thick glaze. Turn the tempeh once as you simmer and spoon over the sauce from time to time.

Serve the tempeh with the sauce. Sprinkle with coriander leaves and a good squeeze of lime juice.

Smoky pork and bean chilli

Serves 6–8

900g/2lb pork shoulder, diced into
2cm/¾ inch cubes

salt and pepper

5 tbsp olive oil

2 large onions, roughly chopped

6 garlic cloves, finely chopped

1 heaped tbsp sweet paprika

1 heaped tbsp ground cumin

1 tsp chipotle paste or Tabasco
sauce

800g/1lb 12oz canned plum
tomatoes, puréed

4 tbsp cider vinegar

40g/1½oz/3¼ tbsp light
brown sugar

550g/1¼lb home-cooked beans,
or 2 x 400g/14oz cans beans
such as black, pinto or borlotti
(cranberry) beans, rinsed

To serve:

red onion, chopped

avocado, chopped

coriander leaves (cilantro),
chopped

grated cheese

boiled rice

Here's a dish to feed a crowd. You can really get ahead of yourself as the chilli will be even better after a couple of days in the refrigerator. The recipe comes from Jennifer Joyce's *Meals in Heels*, a collection of 'do-ahead dishes for the dinner party diva'. Jennifer's food always bursts with gutsy, intense flavours and this is no exception.

Season the pork with salt and pepper. Place a large saucepan with a tablespoon of the olive oil over a medium heat and cook the pork in batches for a minute or two on each side, until browned all over. Set the meat aside.

Turn down the heat, add the remaining oil with the onions and garlic, season with salt and pepper and cook very gently for about 5 minutes, until soft. Add the paprika, cumin and chipotle paste and continue to cook for a couple of minutes.

Now throw in the tomatoes, vinegar, sugar and pork, cover with a lid and cook gently for about 1 hour or until the pork is tender. Add your choice of beans and warm through.

Serve the chilli in bowls, topped with the red onion, avocado, coriander and some grated cheese with boiled rice alongside.

Turkey, chickpea and pistachio pilaf

Serves 4–6

200g/7oz/generous 1 cup basmati rice, soaked in tepid water for 1 hour

300ml/10½fl oz/1¼ cups turkey stock

12 saffron threads, ground with a pestle and mortar

50g/1¾oz/4 tbsp unsalted butter

2 onions, sliced

½ cinnamon stick

3 cardamom pods, bruised

500g/1lb 2oz home-cooked chickpeas (garbanzo beans), or 2 x 400g/14oz cans chickpeas, rinsed

50g/1¾oz/¼ cup sultanas (golden raisins)

salt and pepper

about 250g/9oz cooked turkey meat, shredded

100g/3½oz/generous ¾ cup lightly toasted pistachios, roughly chopped

large bunch of fresh parsley, chopped

seeds and juice of 1 pomegranate

juice of 1 lemon

This spiced pilaf is now a regular in my festive repertoire. A perfect dish for turkey leftovers and equally good with chicken, duck or lamb.

While the rice is soaking, add 2 tablespoons of the stock to the saffron in the mortar and leave to soak.

Heat the butter in a large heavy saucepan (one that has a well-fitting lid), add the onions, cinnamon and cardamom, and cook gently until the onions are completely soft.

Drain the rice and add to the pan, turning it in the butter to coat. Add the chickpeas, sultanas, saffron stock, turkey stock and a touch of salt and pepper.

Cover with a lid and boil for 5 minutes, reduce the heat and simmer for 5 more minutes, and then leave to rest (still covered) for at least 10 minutes.

Fork in the turkey, pistachios, parsley and about half of the pomegranate. Season to taste with salt, pepper and lemon juice. Sprinkle with the remaining pomegranate seeds, tipping over any juices and serve at once.

Master recipe for bean burgers

2 tbsp olive oil, plus extra for frying

1 onion, roughly chopped

2 garlic cloves, crushed

2 x 400g/14oz cans of beans, rinsed, or 500g/1lb 2oz home-cooked beans, such as cannellini, haricot (navy), pinto, black beans, red kidney beans, butter beans (large lima beans) or chickpeas (garbanzos)

2 eggs, beaten

5 tbsp dried breadcrumbs

salt and pepper

To add extra flavour and texture:

chopped nuts, seeds, vegetables, herbs or spices

Heat the oil in a pan over a medium heat and cook the onion until just soft. Add the garlic (and any spices you are using) and cook until you're enveloped in wonderful smells. Set aside.

Purée three-quarters of the beans using a hand-held blender or whizz them in a food processor or just go wild with a potato masher. You want a slightly lumpy, creamy texture. Add the remaining whole beans and the onion and garlic mixture.

Stir in the eggs and breadcrumbs with whatever nuts, seeds, vegetables, herbs or spices you are using. Season with salt and pepper to taste.

Press the mixture into firm cakes. The size is up to you, but I usually make 6. A few hours' chilling in the refrigerator will firm up the burgers before cooking but is not absolutely necessary.

Cooking your burgers

Pan-fry your burgers in olive oil over a medium heat. They will hold together fairly well but be gentle as you turn them over. About 5–6 minutes on each side will do the trick. You can keep them hot in the oven (160°C/325°F/gas mark 3) for about 15 minutes; any longer and they dry out a little.

Alternatively, you can place the burgers on a greased baking sheet, drizzle with a little oil and bake in a hot oven (200°C/400°F/gas mark 6) for about 20 minutes. I usually turn the burgers over to serve, as the underside crusts up nicely.

Californian black bean burgers

master burger recipe (opposite)
made with black beans or a
mixture of black and pinto

1-2 small fresh red chillies, finely
chopped or a large pinch of
cayenne pepper

1 tsp ground cumin

zest of ½ lime

juice of 1 lime

1 tbsp chopped fresh
coriander (cilantro)

2 tbsp sweetcorn kernels

3 tbsp roasted peanuts, roughly
chopped (or sprouted peanuts)

Prepare the master recipe, adding the chillies and
cumin as you cook the garlic. Stir all the remaining
ingredients into your bean mixture.

Follow the preparation and cooking instructions on
the opposite page.

The super burger

master burger recipe (opposite)
made with haricots (navy beans),
cannellini, butter beans (large
lima beans)

4 tbsp cooked quinoa

large handful of sprouting beans

1 tbsp balsamic vinegar

8 sun-dried tomatoes, very
finely chopped

2 tbsp freshly chopped tarragon

Prepare the master recipe and stir in all the super
burger ingredients. Season to taste.

Follow the preparation and cooking instructions on
the opposite page.

To serve, stir the mustard into the crème fraîche and
serve with the burgers.

To serve:

1-2 tbsp grainy French mustard

6 tbsp crème fraîche or soured
oat cream

Celeriac and lentil gratin

Serves 4–6

The nutty celeriac has a wonderful texture and the creamy tomato sauce lends the lentils a touch of luxury.

2 tbsp olive oil
1 onion, finely diced
4 garlic cloves, crushed
2 x 400g/14oz cans of chopped tomatoes
300g/10½oz/1½ cups Castelluccio lentils, rinsed
salt and pepper
large handful of parsley, roughly chopped
225ml/8fl oz double (heavy) cream
1 celeriac, about 1kg/2¼lb, peeled, quartered and finely sliced
zest and juice of ½ lemon
100g/3½oz Parmesan cheese, grated

Preheat the oven to 190°C/375°F/Gas mark 5.

Heat the oil in a large saucepan and cook the onion gently until soft and golden. Add the garlic and stir until its wonderful smell wafts up from the pan. Tip in the tomatoes and simmer for about 10 minutes.

Meanwhile, put the lentils in a pan, cover with about 5cm/2 inches of water and simmer for 20 minutes, until just soft and creamy rather than al dente. Drain if necessary, then season well with salt and pepper. Stir in the parsley and 3 tablespoons of the cream.

Add the celeriac to the tomato sauce, cover and cook for about 15 minutes or until tender. At first, there will not appear to be enough tomato sauce, but the celeriac will release plenty of moisture as it cooks. When the celeriac is tender, add the remaining cream, the lemon zest and juice, and season with salt and plenty of black pepper to taste.

Layer the celeriac and tomato mixture alternately with the lentils in a large, shallow ovenproof dish, finishing with a layer of celeriac. Sprinkle with the grated Parmesan and bake for about 30 minutes.

This can be prepared ahead and even frozen. Thaw before baking for an extra 10–15 minutes, covering with foil if the top begins to get too dark.

Slow-roast shoulder of lamb with flageolet beans

Serves 4–6

Meltingly tender slow-cooked lamb and tiny green flageolet beans are a French classic combination.

2 tbsp olive oil
1.8kg/4lb shoulder of lamb
2 onions, diced
4 garlic cloves, crushed
1 tbsp finely chopped rosemary
½ bottle dry white wine
salt and pepper
700g/1lb 9oz home-cooked flageolets, or 3 x 400g/14oz cans flageolet beans, rinsed
3 leeks, roughly sliced
250g/9oz green beans, topped but not tailed
2 tbsp roughly chopped flat-leaf parsley
dash of balsamic vinegar

Preheat the oven to 170°C/325°F/gas mark 3.

Heat the oil in a large, deep roasting pan or a large cast-iron cooking pot over a high heat and sear the lamb until browned all over. Add the onions, garlic, rosemary, wine and a little salt and pepper. Cover with a well-fitting lid or cover the whole pan carefully with foil (you want to create a steamy environment). Roast for 3 hours, then turn the oven down to 140°C/275°F/gas mark 1 and cook for another 4 hours.

About an hour before serving, remove the pan from the oven and skim off any excess fat. Taste the lamb juices and season with salt and pepper. Add the flageolet beans and leeks to the pan, replace the lid or foil, and cook for a further hour. There should be plenty of liquid for the vegetables to soak up, but do add a little stock or water if it seems dry.

Remove the pan from the oven, lift out the meat and set aside to rest for a few minutes while you steam or boil the green beans until just tender. Add to the flageolets, season well and add the parsley.

You should now be able to break up the tender lamb with a fork. Spoon the beans onto individual plates, and top with the lamb. Add a dash of balsamic vinegar – you need a bit of acidity – and serve.

Smoked haddock, spinach and curried lentils

Serves 4

Smoked haddock has a great affinity with curry flavours, best known in kedgeree.

600g/1lb 5oz smoked haddock fillet, skinned and boned, cut into 4 pieces

juice of 1 lemon

100g/3½oz/7 tbsp unsalted butter

1 onion, diced

1 carrot, diced

2 garlic cloves, crushed

2cm/¾ inch piece of fresh ginger, finely diced

2 stalks of lemongrass, outer leaves removed, very finely diced

1–2 tbsp medium curry powder

100ml/3½fl oz/7 tbsp double (heavy) cream

250g/9oz/1¼ cups small lentils such as pardina, Puy or Castelluccio, well rinsed, cooked

salt and pepper

400g/14oz fresh spinach, washed

2 tbsp olive oil

2 tbsp roughly chopped fresh parsley or coriander (cilantro)

1 lemon, cut into wedges, to serve

Optional topping: 4 poached eggs

Put the fish in a dish and squeeze over the lemon juice, cover, and place in the refrigerator.

Heat half the butter in a saucepan and cook the onion and carrot until the onion is soft. Add the garlic, ginger and lemongrass. Stir for a minute or two, taking care not to burn the garlic, before adding the curry powder. Stir again and then tip in the cream. Pour the curry cream over the cooked lentils, give them a stir, taste and season well.

Cook the spinach in another pan. There will probably be enough moisture from washing the leaves. Cover with a well-fitting lid and cook over a medium heat until the spinach has collapsed. Drain, squeeze well (I love to drink the juice) and season. Too much washing up? Just add the raw spinach to the hot lentils and allow to wilt. A little wetter, not quite as pretty, but hey ho.

Heat the oil and the remaining butter in a large frying pan and pan-fry the haddock until cooked through and beginning to flake – a matter of minutes on each side, depending on the thickness of the fish.

Place a mound of lentils on each plate, then some spinach and crown with the fish. Sprinkle with parsley or coriander and serve with lemon wedges.

Smoky prawns with chickpeas

Serves 4

Just a few indulgent prawns go a very long way.

16–24 shell-on raw prawns (shrimp)

4 tbsp olive oil

1 onion, diced

2 potatoes, diced and cooked until tender

500g/1lb 2oz home-cooked chickpeas (garbanzo beans), or 2 x 400g/14oz cans chickpeas, rinsed

salt

1 tbsp hot smoked paprika

75ml/2½fl oz/5 tbsp dry white wine

200g/7oz cherry tomatoes, halved

2 tbsp roughly chopped flat-leaf parsley

4 lemon slices, to serve

Remove the heads from the prawns and place them in a small saucepan with 1 tablespoon of the oil. Fry off the heads until they begin to turn pink and then add 3 tablespoons of water. Now you need to crush the heads to release all the fabulous flavour. You can use a mouli legumes, a potato masher and then push the juices through a sieve, or a potato ricer, which looks like a giant garlic press. Set aside the deep orange, prawny juices.

Heat 2 tablespoons of the oil in a large pan, ideally something you can put on the table, and cook the onion until soft. Add the diced potatoes, chickpeas, a pinch of salt and the prawn juices, and stir around carefully. Leave over a low heat.

Sprinkle the prawns with the smoked paprika. Heat the remaining oil in another large frying pan and throw in the prawns. As soon as you can really smell the paprika, it's time to add the wine and the cherry tomatoes. Cook until the prawns are just firm and the flesh is opaque.

Tip the prawns, tomatoes and juices over the chickpeas, sprinkle with parsley, taste and season. Serve with a slice of lemon. Generous quantities of aioli are good, too. You can worry about the garlic later (Campari works wonders).

Sweet Treats

Noah's pudding

Serves 8–10

200g/7oz/1 rounded cup wheat berries, soaked overnight

50g/1¾oz/¼ cup dried chickpeas (garbanzo beans), soaked overnight

115g/4oz/¾ cup dried haricot (navy), cannellini or butter beans (large lima beans) – a mixture is ideal – soaked overnight

50g/1¾oz/¼ cup sultanas, currants or raisins – or a mixture

12 dried apricots, roughly chopped

6 dried figs, stems removed, roughly chopped

50g/1¾oz/¼ cup short-grain pudding rice

100g/3½oz/¾ cup walnuts, blanched almonds and skinned hazelnuts (ideally a few of each), roughly chopped

280g/10oz/1½ cups caster (superfine) sugar

zest of ½ lemon or orange, sliced into very fine strips

2–4 tbsp rosewater

For the top:

seeds from 1 pomegranate

3 tbsp roughly chopped pistachios, almonds or pine nuts

1 tbsp toasted sesame seeds

A legendary dessert that I first stumbled upon in *The Independent Cook* by Jeremy Round. The pudding is an unlikely combination of pulses, wheat, rice and dried fruit that Noah is said to have scraped together from the last provisions left on the Ark as the floodwaters subsided.

Put the wheat berries in a large pot with 2.5 litres/ 4½ pints/2½ quarts cold water, bring to the boil and then simmer for about 1 hour, or until the grains have become quite soft (some wheat berries take longer).

Meanwhile, cook the chickpeas and beans in separate pots until tender (see pages 18–19) and drain.

Soak all the dried fruit in warm water to cover.

Once the wheat is cooked, remove a few spoonfuls with some of the cooking liquid and purée with a hand-held blender. Add the purée and the rice to the wheat berries and boil for about 15 minutes, stirring from time to time. Add more water if the pudding seems too thick and sticky.

Throw in the cooked beans and chickpeas, soaked fruit and the nuts. Stir in three-quarters of the sugar and strips of zest and simmer for about 20 minutes.

Add a little water or milk if the pudding seems very thick (it will set as it cools) and remove from the heat. Add the rosewater and the remaining sugar (or some honey if you prefer) to taste. Leave to cool. Sprinkle with pomegranate seeds, pistachios and sesame seeds and serve.

Black bean brownies

West Coast Americans got into a frenzy of excitement about gluten-free beany brownies a couple of years ago, here's why.

140g/5oz/generous ½ cup unsalted butter, cut into small cubes, plus extra for greasing

200g/7oz dark chocolate, broken into small pieces

1 tbsp unsweetened cocoa powder

2 tsp vanilla extract

1 x 400g/14oz can black beans or 250g/9oz home-cooked black beans

3 eggs

85g/3oz roughly chopped walnuts, pecans, pistachios or almonds

200g/7oz/1 cup caster (superfine) sugar

1 tsp sea salt, for sprinkling

Preheat the oven to 180°C/350°F/Gas mark 4. Butter a 24cm/9½ inch square baking pan or line with parchment paper.

Melt the chocolate and butter together in a large heatproof bowl placed over a pan of simmering water or in the microwave on low. Leave to cool a little, then add the cocoa and vanilla.

Meanwhile, blend the beans with one of the eggs in a food processor or using a hand-held blender. The mixture should be as smooth as possible, otherwise the brownies will have a mealy texture. Gradually stir the bean mixture and the nuts into the melted chocolate.

Beat the remaining eggs with the sugar until light and creamy, and then fold into the brownie mixture.

Pour into the pan, sprinkle with salt and bake for about 25–30 minutes, until just set but still a little wobbly. Place the pan on a wire rack and leave to cool completely before attempting to cut up into small squares. (If the brownies seem very gooey, placing them in the refrigerator for half an hour will make them easier to slice.) In the unlikely event of leftovers, you can keep the brownies in an airtight container for up to 5 days.

Adzuki bean ice cream with crystallized ginger

Serves 4

For the red bean paste:

200g/7oz/1 cup adzuki beans

175g/6oz/generous ¾ cup caster (superfine) sugar

good pinch of salt

about 50g/1¾oz crystallized ginger, cut into wafer-thin slices, to serve

For the ice cream:

570ml/1 pint/scant 2½ cups full-fat milk

300ml/10½fl oz/1¼ cups double (heavy) cream

225g/8oz/generous 1 cup caster (superfine) sugar

8 egg yolks (yes, it's time for a meringue frenzy)

few drops of vanilla extract

Adzuki beans are incredibly popular throughout East Asia. They are cooked in some savoury dishes, such as the Japanese sticky rice and red bean dish, *sekihan*, that's served at special occasions, but mostly they are eaten as a sweet paste. Red bean paste turns up in all manner of confectionery, pastries and desserts. It's the chocolate of East Asia. I've tried it in a few traditional incarnations, such as Chinese mooncakes and delicate Japanese rice cakes – I'd say they're an acquired taste! But bring on this ice cream, with its Filipino heritage, and I'm smitten.

To make the red bean paste: put the beans in a pan of cold water and bring to the boil, turn off the heat and leave for 5 minutes and then drain. (Purists repeat this process, but I found no noticeable difference when I did a taste test.)

Start again and this time simmer the beans until tender, around 40 minutes–1 hour. The beans should still be whole but will squash to a creamy paste between your fingers. At this stage, the beans should still just be submerged in water.

Add the sugar and salt (some recipes call for equal quantities of beans and sugar, so if you have a really sweet tooth, go ahead) and stir the beans as they simmer. Mash with the back of a spoon and cook until the sugary water has almost disappeared.

Drag a spoon across the bottom of the pan; it should leave a clear track. Now you can blitz the beans in a blender to make them smooth or leave them textured, as I prefer; both are traditional. Spoon the paste into a bowl to cool.

To make the ice cream: put the milk, cream and sugar in a pan and slowly bring to the boil. Don't leave the pan, or it will suddenly froth up.

Meanwhile, beat the egg yolks and vanilla together in a large bowl. Pour the scalding-hot milk mixture over the yolks, whisking all the time, and then strain the mixture back into the pan. Stir over a low heat until the mixture thickens enough to coat the back of a spoon and then tip back into the bowl.

Whisk in about 250g/9oz of the red bean paste and leave to cool. Pour the cooled mixture into an ice-cream maker to churn. Freeze until ready to serve.

The remaining bean paste can be frozen for your next batch of ice-cream, or sandwiched between tiny Scotch (American-style) pancakes.

Serve in bowls with slithers of crystallized ginger.

Chickpea, chocolate and lime energy balls

Prep 35 minutes
Makes 20

The perfect snack when you're after a healthy energy boost. These little balls may taste rather indulgent but they're packed with protein and fibre, as well as natural sugars, meaning that you'll be, quite literally, full of beans for hours. The balls take a matter of minutes to make and will keep in the refrigerator for up to a week.

250g/9oz home-cooked chickpeas (garbanzo beans), or 400g/14oz can chickpeas, drained and rinsed

100g/3½oz/¾ cup pitted dates

60g/2oz/¼ cup peanut butter

3 tbsp cocoa powder

zest of 1 lime

½ tsp ground cinnamon

1-2 tsp vanilla extract

2-3 tbsp maple syrup

4 tbsp toasted pumpkin seeds

½ tsp chilli flakes (optional)

6 tbsp unsweetened desiccated (shredded) coconut

Blitz the chickpeas, dates, peanut butter, cocoa, lime zest, cinnamon and a teaspoon of the vanilla extract together in a food processor. Now give it a taste before you add the maple syrup; your dates may be very sweet, in which case you may choose to add less maple syrup, or even to leave it out altogether. Vanilla extract can vary in intensity too, so gauge if you need a drop more or not.

Add the toasted pumpkin seeds and the chilli flakes, if you like a little heat, then pulse the mixture a few times, aiming to retain some of the crunchy texture.

Put the coconut in a separate bowl. Roll the chickpea mixture between your palms into walnut-size balls (you should get about 20), before turning them over in the coconut to cover. Place the balls in the refrigerator for 30 minutes to firm up.

Pulsating Smoothies

It might seem bonkers to be throwing beans into your morning smoothie but the pulses add a wonderful creaminess to the mix and you'll benefit from the added fibre and protein too, keeping you full for hours. You can freeze the beans (home-cooked or canned) in a ziplock bag so that you can just grab a handful and throw them into any smoothie you happen to be making. Drain the pulses and freeze on a tray before bagging up, to stop them clumping together.

Mango, ginger and white bean

Prep 5 minutes
Makes 1

60g/2oz/scant ½ cup cooked and drained haricot (navy) beans

1 mango, peeled and pitted

2 oranges, peeled and deseeded

1cm/½ inch piece of fresh ginger, roughly chopped

zest and juice of ½–1 lime

6 ice cubes

Whizz everything together in a blender until smooth and fabulously creamy.

Strawberry, blueberry and chickpea

Prep 5 minutes
Makes 1

60g/2oz/scant ½ cup cooked and drained chickpeas (garbanzo beans)

200g/7oz/2 cups strawberries

100g/3½oz/¾ cup blueberries

½ tsp vanilla extract

6 ice cubes

1 tsp honey or maple syrup (optional)

Put the chickpeas, fruit, vanilla and ice in a blender and blitz until smooth. Taste and sweeten with honey or maple syrup if desired. If your strawberries are very ripe, you may not need to sweeten.

If the smoothie seems too thick, just add a little apple juice or milk or whizz with a few extra ice cubes.

Index

Acknowledgements

For Libbus, you're super human, I'm so proud of you.

Huge thanks to everyone at Pavilion, including Stephanie Milner, Laura Brodie, Komal Patel, Katie Cowan and Polly Powell. Special thanks to Emily Preece-Morrison who embraced my idea from the outset and made this book come true. To Maggie Ramsay, Nicola Graimes and Sarah Epton, for your meticulous editing, patience and being fun with it all too.

To all of you who've made this book look stunning, leaving the hippy hessian right out of the picture. To Georgina Hewitt for dealing with all those tiny pulse shots, and to Laura Russell and Emily Breen for the stunning layout. And then for the simply amazing photos: I am so grateful to stylist Wei Tang, to Maud Eden for cooking the dishes so beautifully, to Natalie Costaras for keeping everything running smoothly and to super-talented photographer Clare Winfield for your fabulous vision.

To Hannah Cameron McKenna for all your invaluable recipe testing.

To every cook, chef, food writer and friend who's kindly shared a recipe: Richard Bertinet, Sarah Britton, Clara Grace Paul and Barney McGrath. And to those who have allowed me to re-publish a recipe: Jude Blereau from *Coming Home to Eat – Wholefood for the Family* (Murdoch Books, 2008) and Jennifer Joyce from *Meals in Heels* (Murdoch Books, 2010). To everyone I work with at Books for Cooks, Divertimenti, Leiths and The Bertinet Kitchen for wise words and great encouragement.

To all my eager Bristol guinea pigs who often sampled half a dozen pulse experiments at a time, sometimes with the predictable after effects.

To my family: Mum, Richard and Libbus, you've been unbelievably supportive. Lastly, I'm infinitely grateful to my wonderful Peter and little Imi for keeping me sane (and miraculously remaining so yourselves too) through months of experimentation, endless beany buffets, a chaotic kitchen, wobbles, triumphs and deadlines.